W0114306

OCTOBER 7TH

BOOKS BY MARSHA LEDERMAN

Kiss the Red Stairs

October 7th

SEARCHING FOR THE
HUMANITARIAN MIDDLE

Marsha Lederman

McCLELLAND & STEWART

McClelland & Stewart and colophon are registered trademarks of Penguin Random House Canada Limited.

The authorized representative in the EU for product safety and compliance is Penguin Random House Ireland, Morrison Chambers, 32 Nassau Street, Dublin D02 YH68, Ireland, https://eu-contact.penguin.ie

Library and Archives Canada Cataloguing in Publication

Title: October 7th : a year in conflict from the humanitarian middle / Marsha Lederman.
Other titles: October seventh
Names: Lederman, Marsha (Western arts correspondent), author
Identifiers: Canadiana (print) 20250117428 | Canadiana (ebook) 20250117436 | ISBN 9780771024146 (hardcover) | ISBN 9780771024153 (EPUB)
Subjects: LCSH: October 7 Hamas Attack, Israel, 2023. | LCSH: Israel-Hamas War, 2023- | LCSH: Israeli-Palestinian conflict—1993-—Social aspects. | LCSH: Jews, Israeli—Social conditions. | LCSH: Palestinian Arabs—Gaza Strip—Social conditions. | LCSH: War and society—Israel. | LCSH: War and society—Gaza Strip. | LCSH: Antisemitism—Social aspects.
Classification: LCC DS119.77 .L43 2025 | DDC 956.94/3055—dc23

These columns and articles were originally published in *The Globe and Mail*. © Copyright 2025 The Globe and Mail Inc. All Rights Reserved. globeandmail.com and *The Globe and Mail* are divisions of The Globe and Mail Inc.

Excerpt(s) from THE ZONE OF INTEREST: A NOVEL by Martin Amis, copyright © 2014 by Martin Amis. Used by permission of Alfred A. Knopf, an imprint of the Knopf Doubleday Publishing Group, a division of Penguin Random House LLC. All rights reserved.

Cover design by Talia Ambramson
Cover art: Talia Abramson
Typeset in Arno Pro by Terra Page
Printed in Canada

McClelland & Stewart
A division of Penguin Random House Canada
320 Front Street West, Suite 1400
Toronto, Ontario, M5V 3B6, Canada
penguinrandomhouse.ca

1 2 3 4 5   29 28 27 26 25

Penguin
Random House
McCLELLAND & STEWART

For the victims of October 7th, 2023,
and the catastrophe that followed.

And for their families.

CONTENTS

INTRODUCTION

When the October 7th attacks occurred on that Saturday morning in Israel, it was very late Friday on the west coast of Canada, where I live. It was still October 6th, 2023. I had been to a Vancouver Canucks pre-season game with my son and a friend. The Canucks won; even for a lifelong Toronto Maple Leafs fan like me, it was a good night. It was Thanksgiving weekend, and my son was about to turn fifteen.

I have come to think of that evening as my last normal night.

Like many children of Holocaust survivors, I have, since childhood, had regular nightmares about being hunted by Nazis. That weekend, what I had previously tried to consider a ludicrous, irrational fear came to life. I watched it on social media. The Nazis of my nightmares had turned into Hamas terrorists.

I wrote a whole book about how intergenerational trauma has affected me—separation anxiety; a tremendous pessimism; a tendency to catastrophize; a fear, even in happy times, that the other shoe is always about to drop.

And then it dropped. On October 7th, 2023. And if I thought my inherited trauma had been an issue before, well, that was nothing. This invasion went even deeper, seeping into every aspect of my life. I began to exist in a state of tremendous anxiety and fear, worried about things that would never have given me pause in the Before Times.

The antisemitism reached a level I never would have expected to witness in my lifetime. On social media, university campuses, at workplaces. As a reporter writing about this, I would become a repository for other people's stories. Almost daily, someone would reach out about an internal memo with antisemitic undertones (or worse), an uncomfortable customer service experience, antisemitism at their child's school. I could go on. I was shocked by what I was hearing—from people in the education system, health care, the arts.

On October 7th, I knew immediately that Israel would retaliate, that it would be terrible for Gaza, and that there would be repercussions globally with a rise in anti-Israel sentiment. But even I, Queen Catastrophizer, did not expect things to escalate as they did. Even I, clear-eyed, glass-half-empty pragmatist, did not expect the war to be what it became.

My question for myself that Thanksgiving weekend, professionally, as an Opinion columnist for a national newspaper, *The Globe and Mail*, was: Did I want to write about what was going on in Israel, to weigh in on as public a forum as I could imagine?

On this terrible thing that had happened, and was happening? (It seems crazy now that I even asked myself that question, given how this story would come to dominate the headlines for a year and well beyond.)

I thought: *Whatever I write, whatever I say, I am going to get it. I am possibly going to get it from all sides. It will be pointed out that I am Jewish and the argument will be that I'm too biased to write about this.* But also, I am a progressive, liberal Jew, who is already on record as being opposed to the government of Benjamin Netanyahu. I consider myself a humanist and have always desperately wanted peace with the Palestinians and dignity and security for all. I regret to write that I knew some members of the Jewish community would not be comfortable with my opinions on this matter either. It felt inevitable that I would anger people on all points of this tricky spectrum.

And, as you will read, I did.

Did I really need this? Could I handle it? My intergenerational trauma had already been triggered in such a profound way. But I couldn't stay silent.

I chose to work in the field of journalism in part because of a noble, if incredibly naive, belief. I thought if reporters had been able to tell the story of what was happening in Nazi Germany and then during the full-blown Holocaust, the genocide could have been prevented or curtailed. Lives could have been saved. Maybe my grandparents' lives. I never got to meet them.

But what I learned is that reporters did tell these stories. These stories were published in *The Globe and Mail*, the *New York Times* and elsewhere. And nothing happened. Well, everything happened. It was allowed to happen. So journalists can't always change the world. Still, we can never stop trying. Otherwise, what's the point?

Believe me, there were many times over that year, especially in the first dizzying months, when I thought: *Just stop. Step away. Write about something else* (as I often did, I should state). *Leave this to others with less skin in the game.*

But I felt I had a responsibility to write about this terrible time—for Palestinians, for Israelis, and for Jews and Muslims in the diaspora. I sat alone on early mornings and late nights at my dining room table, reading the catastrophic news from the Middle East, reading open letters that intensified my isolation, writing about what I could. I lit a candle in the window for the hostages. I drank a lot of coffee.

I am trying to remember now when I stopped lighting that candle every dark morning. When the loss and horror became so everyday that it threatened to become routine. What was my candle going to do for the hostages? Or the thousands of dead Gazans?

We all deserve peace. Palestinians, Israelis, and the rest of us. As I wrote, I struggled with terminology. Who did I mean when I talked about the "other side," exactly? "Pro-Palestinian" didn't feel like the right term for some of what I was seeing. I am pro-Palestinian. So are many Jewish people who participate in pro-Palestinian protests. And many of us who don't. Palestinians deserve good, safe lives, just as Israelis do. They deserve homes, food, equality. Security. Life! They did not deserve the war. Or the displacement and persecution they have experienced for decades. But I was infuriated at how the Hamas terrorists who went into Israel and murdered and raped and took people—children!—hostage were being held up as freedom fighters, as noble resistance. Including by feminists and other progressives I have been aligned with on other important issues. I couldn't believe what I was witnessing. I could not understand it.

I did my best to reflect my values in the pieces that I did write, values that are rooted in my Jewish upbringing—and that stem from the "never again" mantra that I also grew up with. Never again—for anyone.

There are things I would probably change if I was writing these pieces today, but for this collection we wanted to capture, unvarnished, the sense of that time as it unfolded. There are statistics, including death counts, that are now out of date or inaccurate, but the columns appear with their original publication dates so the time period the numbers reflect should be clear. There are contradictions across the columns as information continued to change. But we kept them as we published them to accurately reflect the writing of the time. (We did correct a few typos and other copy errors, as well as making minor alterations to ensure clarity, avoid repetition, and conform to McClelland & Stewart style. We also removed some specific details [dates, venues] regarding artistic performances. In some rare instances, I changed direct quotes to paraphrases, but these were the only changes we made.) In places where I thought some additional, or updated, information would be useful, I've included a footnote or postscript. We've added a bit of information preceding each piece to situate the reader in the conflict at that time.

In the first section of this collection, we have reproduced the pieces I wrote about the attack, the war, and the surprising rise in antisemitism (well, I was surprised) that followed until the end of 2023. They are in chronological order, so as to capture what it felt like as things developed. If I went back and reflected on that time, the sentiments would no doubt require some adjustment, altered by what we all know, and feel, now. We didn't want to do that; our objective was to communicate that volatile time through a contemporaneous lens.

Part three of the book resumes this format: again, trying to capture the feeling of what was happening as the calendar flipped to 2024, through to the first anniversary of the attacks.

In the middle part of this collection, we have included a few pieces I had previously written for *The Globe* that deal with Jewish identity. These pieces, I hope, offer a lens into the Jewish-Canadian experience—including my own—that exists outside the war which is currently raging, as I write this.

These pieces were a surprise, even to me, as I compiled them. I have written far more about Jewish identity than I had thought. It was something I believed I had rarely referenced in my work. I was wrong about that.

This goes back to the first piece I ever wrote, as a freelancer, for *The Globe and Mail*, the newspaper that would later become my professional home and in many ways my life. It was about a trip to Poland that I took in 1998 with my mother, sisters, a cousin, and my niece. I called it "Going Home to Auschwitz." Imagining being in that place with my mother, who had survived the concentration camp, was excruciating and empowering. An educational publisher reproduced that essay for a language arts textbook. I still hear from students, occasionally, who have read it and want to ask me questions or share their thoughts. These letters are very special to me.

There was little after that essay that reflected my Jewish heritage—until a 2012 encounter with the celebrated German-Canadian artist Fred Herzog. In my initial draft of that story, which was about some shocking things he had said to me about the Holocaust during an interview about his life and photography, I had included only one line about my own background: "(Both of my parents were Holocaust survivors.)" One parenthetical thought.

But my editor at the time had a vision: the fact that of all the people Herzog could have said these things to, he had said them to me. My editor felt that my story was an important element, and so we made the decision to include it. I thought of that as my "coming out" as a journalist who was Jewish. We called it "The Collision."

And then, in 2022, I published a memoir about inter-generational trauma and the Holocaust, further solidifying my identity—whether I had wanted to or not—as a Jewish journalist. Had I not written that book, I might have felt less comfortable writing anything that referenced my Jewish identity, but the jig was up, and so I continued.

It set the stage, in a way, for everything I have written since October 7th 2023. In those first few months, I felt like I had gone from a journalist who happened to be Jewish to a Jewish journalist. I was not very comfortable with that shift in perception. Or, frankly, with how I started viewing myself. There were collisions all around.

Many pieces about art comprise part two of this collection, as my job for fifteen years at *The Globe* was to write about the arts. Another surprise to me: almost every piece here is related to the Holocaust in some way. I should say that in no way should this be interpreted as any sort of justification for the war in Gaza. These are separate issues, although the founding of the State of Israel was very much connected to the horrors of the Holocaust, as you will read in the introduction to the second part of this collection. I was also struck by this: how eerily some of these pieces foreshadowed the war between Israel and Hamas that I would write about, years later, repeatedly.

I should also state that I am in no way asserting myself as a voice for Jewish Canadians, journalists or Jews in general. The Jewish community is diverse and not at all homogenous; there is a huge range of opinions on this issue and on all matters, including within tight family units. These are my personal thoughts and opinions. Sometimes, as you will read, they do get very personal.

At the same time, they *are* personal. This writing comes from a very particular point of view. I was observing all of this as a Jewish person in the diaspora—alarmed by the October 7th, 2023 attacks, alarmed by the antisemitism which resulted in Canada and around the world. I was also gutted and furious about the victims of the war in Gaza. That pain has been searing. Even if I was accused again and again of not caring. I cared, and care, deeply.

These columns were written specifically from my point of view as a progressive Canadian Jew who believes in a two-state solution. They were complemented by a lot of excellent writing in *The Globe and Mail* by Palestinians, Muslims and other humanitarians with a wide range of differing opinions. I hope you will seek that out too.

As a Jewish journalist, I suppose it was inevitable that Canadian Jews began reaching out to me with stories of the antisemitism they had been experiencing. Very few people were contacting me to talk about Islamophobia. I wasn't the go-to person for that, understandably. (Although I am equally outraged by those stories.) So, in these pieces, the experience of antisemitism during this period is reflected to a much greater extent and dominates the narrative. It is also something I had personal experience with.

And in my current role, as a columnist, my job is to write opinion pieces rather than to straight-up report the news itself.

My search for the humanitarian middle is, as I write, a very personal one. These columns in no way constitute a comprehensive overall accounting of that first year; they are my observations and my opinions. What I have written was informed not just by the horrible events, but by my own background and history; there is no question that my writing was steeped in my own life experiences.

I was raised in a very Jewish enclave of Toronto, in a warm home that was nonetheless heavy with the weight of what had happened to my parents. They were Holocaust survivors and their parents—my grandparents—were murdered in gas chambers. This dark history was always present, in some way; it was part of our identity. We observed the holidays, were (mostly) kosher in the home, attended an orthodox synagogue. My parents often spoke to each other in Yiddish (and Polish, when they really didn't want us to understand what they were talking about). Still, we were primarily cultural, rather than religiously observant, Jews. It was—and is—a huge part of who I am.

We were also raised on an idyllic idea of Israel. It was portrayed to us as a magical place, our ancestral homeland that had become a geographic saviour for our people after the terrible events earlier in the 20th Century.

This is what we were taught at Hebrew school as well, which I attended part-time, three sessions a week. There, we learned about the history of Israel, but it was from a very particular perspective. We were never told about what happened to the Palestinians as the State of Israel was established. We were taught this history as if it were a story with a happy ending.

One of my teachers would give us points for each correct answer we gave in class, whatever the subject. Accumulate a certain number of points and you would win a prize. The prize was often an Israeli tourism brochure.

When I was nine, my parents took the first overseas trip they would make during my lifetime—to Israel, of course. They came back full of wonder and stories of the land, and of how our relatives were faring there. I couldn't wait to go there myself, which I did, at the age of 18. I spent a summer there working on a kibbutz and travelling around. As I was mourning the unexpected death of my father the previous year, Israel came to the rescue. That summer was healing for me. And it was very fun. And, I know now, formative.

I write in the pieces in this collection about how complex the history is in this part of the world (as it is in any part of the world) and how it has been simplified to the point of absurdity. We often hear about these simplifications from the "pro-Palestinian" "side" (again, I put these terms in quotation marks, because I reject the idea that there are two distinct "sides" and that those who support the existence of a state of Israel, like me, are therefore anti-Palestinian). But on the other "side," many of us were also raised on a simplified story; one that left out the experience of, yes, the other side.

That said, I believe strongly in Jewish self-determination, and Israel's right to exist. I disagree strongly with how it has been existing: the Occupation, the settlements, the perpetual agony of Palestinians in Gaza and the West Bank. The displacement, the violence, the racism, the humiliating treatment. It is wrong.

My hope is for a two-state solution. This is not everyone's hope, I know.

Believing in Israel's right to exist makes me a Zionist, which has become a very dirty word in some circles. I consider myself a progressive Zionist, which many would call an oxymoron. I disagree. I call for change in Israel and I call for an independent Palestine alongside it. Many disagree with that position as well. There is a lot of disagreement in all of this, everywhere. Friendships have ended over it.

I consider myself human first. I am horrified at all that we have lost in this terrible war: the lives, first and foremost. God wept. We all should.

The other loss for me, personally, has been profound: The feeling of safety and security. The comfort of never having to worry about being judged because of the family I was born to, the ethnicity I was born into, the beautiful culture I was so fortunate to inherit. The loss of that feels like a death of something, a great betrayal. It has been shattering.

Over this period, some people reached out and told me that my writing was helping them process the cataclysm. Perhaps putting it all together in one place will help illustrate, help us remember, what that first year was like, beginning with those first awful days.

PART ONE

October 7th

~

I don't know how we come back from this.
Or where we go.

Two days after the initial Hamas attacks.

If you're wondering how your Jewish friends were doing over the Thanksgiving weekend, I know I shouldn't really speak for the lot of us, but: not well.

Canadian Jews—and everyone else—awoke to the stunning news of an invasion by Hamas into Israel. The images were too much to bear. Little children and elderly people—including a Holocaust survivor in a wheelchair—rounded up and taken hostage. A woman's naked body being paraded through the streets on the back of a pickup truck. Families kidnapped and taken to Gaza. The crimes recorded on video for maximum humiliation.

And then, oh my God, the music festival. Dead young people, everywhere. Slaughtered. Parents desperately searching for their missing kids. Living their worst nightmare.

On Facebook, personal accounts from friends of friends and others in Jewish communities were excruciating. One described what happened to a woman's Israeli grandmother: "A terrorist came home to her, killed her, took her phone, filmed the horror, and published it on her Facebook wall. This is how we found out."

The known death toll in Israel stands at more than eight hundred people. October 7th's casualties amounted to the most Jews killed in a single day since the Holocaust. All in one very small country.

It was immediately clear what would come next: an Israeli bombardment on Gaza, where hundreds of innocent people have now already died as a result. All in one tiny territory.

On the Monday following the attacks, the Israeli military ordered a blockade of food, fuel, and electricity to Gaza, where life is already miserable for so many people who had nothing to do with these attacks.

The attacks were carried out by Hamas, which the Canadian government lists as a terrorist organization and whose founding charter called for the destruction of the State of Israel.

Over the weekend of October 7th, social media was flooded by messages of Canadian support for Israel—from the prime minister and premiers, opposition leaders, community leaders.

But also, something else. Videos of people celebrating. The barbaric murder of civilians was being commended as resistance, the cruelty applauded. Not just in Gaza or the West Bank. Here, in Canada.

And then there were the justifications and victim blaming. One Canadian journalist I follow on X wrote about the need for context, whether you "agree with the tactics or not."

Who would agree with the tactic of taking children and old women hostage? Murdering them?

On Saturday, in a now-deleted post on X, a union representing academic workers at McMaster University celebrated the attacks: "Palestine is rising, long live the resistance," followed by a flower emoji. (When I contacted CUPE Local 3906 to inquire, I received an out-of-office message.) Meanwhile, at Harvard, more than thirty student organizations released a statement saying Israel was "entirely responsible" for the unfolding violence. Imagine being a Jewish student, professor, or employee at these schools.

The dislocation and oppression of Palestinian people is despised by many liberal Jews like myself—in Israel and in the diaspora. Many Canadian Jews support a State of Israel but oppose, even loathe, the current government. The hardline, anti-democratic, right-wing government of Benjamin Netanyahu has brought tens of thousands of Israelis into the streets to protest.

But to hold triumphant pro-Palestinian rallies while bullet-ridden bodies are still lying in Israeli streets, shot-up cars, and invaded homes? While their families are still searching for their loved ones? This feels like more than a betrayal.

It feels scary.

For some, the events of the past three days have been triggering. Many Jews are descended from Holocaust survivors, victims of pogroms, and other violent campaigns against our ancestors who were targeted because they were Jewish. My parents were Holocaust survivors, and I promise you the inherited trauma is real. I have spent my life having nightmares about being hunted, hiding for my life.

We tell ourselves we are not being rational; the Holocaust was long ago, and we are safe and under no threat. We, maybe with the help of professionals, try to calm our irrational, epigenetically altered minds.

And then we see Jews being rounded up, humiliated, and slaughtered. Just like our ancestors were.

I know this sounds bizarre, but trust me, this is a real thing. I wrote a whole book about it.

So, no, your Jewish friends are not doing okay.

Your Palestinian friends, who are also the victims of inter-generational and current trauma, are not doing okay either. They are bracing for what's to come. It's going to be awful.

It is awful. For all of us.

Shalom. Salaam. Peace.

OCTOBER 12TH, 2023

Israeli forces have begun air strikes in Gaza.

"Someone's taking photos of your house," a friend called out to me upstairs, from my living room.

No big deal, right?

Although, after October 7th, it was. Why was a stranger taking pictures of the place where I live?

I was immediately anxious. Paranoia? The result of sleep deprivation caused by very terrible world events? Or justified?

In addition to the not-sleeping, the endless doom scrolling, and the almost physical pain of reading about what has been done and is being done to innocent civilians in Israel and Gaza, it has been a terrible time for Canadian Jews. I know—we are free, fed, and sheltered. We are safe.

But we are heartbroken.

And there have been moments when some of us haven't felt so safe. Some of the response to the murders of innocent civilians in Israel has only intensified the insecurity. And the heartbreak.

Before a Vancouver solidarity gathering to show support for Israel, the synagogue I belong to sent out an email with safety instructions, including advice to travel in groups and not to wear obvious identifiers. "Please consider displaying Israeli flags only at the gathering." That did not make me feel safe.

Nor did a photo of the Jewish Community Centre of Greater Vancouver with police cars out front, posted online by a parent picking up their child at the daycare there.

Members of the Jewish community in general have been advised to keep their kids off social media—even to remove Instagram and TikTok from their phones—with the expectation that Hamas could post videos of hostages being executed, as the terrorist group had warned it would do.

How do you tell your teen or tween to stay off TikTok for this particular reason without scaring the daylights out of them? We are trying to protect our children physically and emotionally without scarring them for life.

I have spent far too much time online and seen images of death and terror that I wish I could forget.

But the celebrations and glorification of the murders have been the hardest to take. Along with the justifications of these atrocities as legitimate resistance.

"Gas the Jews!" people shouted at a pro-Palestinian rally in Sydney, Australia. "Boycott Israel" read a (non-sanctioned) sign displayed, briefly, in the window of a Lush store in Dublin.

Student groups, including at the University of Toronto Mississauga, have issued statements that many in the Jewish community have found deeply hurtful. Also some unions—including CUPE Ontario and the union representing some U.S. Starbucks stores.

On a Vancouver Facebook group, a Jewish health care worker asked, despairing, what to do about colleagues posting an image that seemed to celebrate the slaughter—the same illustration of a Palestinian parachute posted (and since deleted) by the Chicago Black Lives Matter organization. (Some Hamas terrorists entered Israel by paraglider; you can see them in the distant sky in videos of the desert dance party.)

Then there was the now-former Air Canada pilot whose "unacceptable posts," as the airline called them, included, according to reports, a sign at a pro-Palestinian rally in Montreal telling Israel, "Hitler is proud of you."

I'm trying to think of another time when innocent civilians were slaughtered, murdered in the most barbaric of ways, hunted house to house—little kids, elderly women, babies—and the so-called progressives of the world (of which I consider myself one) have fallen over themselves to blame the victims.

"Now as ever, we recognize the root cause and ongoing perpetrator of violence in Palestine to be Israeli settler-colonialism and apartheid," read an email from publisher Haymarket Books. This landed in my inbox on Wednesday, after the world had learned of the horrific massacre at a kibbutz.

And now, it is devastating to watch the destruction in Gaza.

And to imagine what is next—for the innocent people there, for all the victims and their families, for the world.

Since moving to Vancouver from Toronto, I've become used to the Jewish community being overlooked. I was irritated this fall when two major cultural organizations—BC and Yukon Book Prizes and the Audain Prize for the Visual Arts—scheduled award ceremonies on Yom Kippur, the holiest day on the Jewish calendar.

These are annoyances. *Jews don't count*, I sometimes tell myself, borrowing the title of David Baddiel's excellent book.

But what's happening now doesn't just feel like we're being ignored. It feels like something much worse.

U.S. president Joe Biden arrives in Israel, but a planned
summit with Arab leaders is cancelled following a deadly
hospital explosion in Gaza the previous day.

Israel's national anthem is called "Hatikvah": "The hope."

It's hard to feel any hope at this moment, with so many deaths.

When it was adopted as the anthem, "Hatikvah" symbolized hope for this refuge rising from the ashes of the Holocaust; hope for the survivors who had experienced so much brutality and for Jews expelled from other Middle Eastern countries; hope for a democracy that would ensure that Jews would have a safe place to go. We say "never again" about the Holocaust—and that statement implies the possibility of an again.

The anthem is based on an 1878 poem by Naftali Herz Imber, a Jewish poet who lived in eastern Europe before leaving for Palestine. The poem communicated a hope to return to the land of the Jewish people after two thousand years of displacement.

Israel, established after the United Nations' 1947 partition plan for Mandatory Palestine, is a tiny nation in the midst of countries that have been, or remain today, hostile to it, with some even denying its right to exist. Its strong army has been essential to its survival, as it has fought neighbouring enemies in wars including the surprise attack on Yom Kippur in 1973.

Fifty years later, the October 7th attack was not a military operation: it was a campaign of cruelty. In addition to the more than 1,400 murders, around 200 people were taken hostage, including children and babies.

The horrific tactics have shaken Israelis, as well as Jews and other feeling people around the world, to the core. For some, that has led to justified anger.

On CNN, an unnamed Israeli soldier was interviewed at Kibbutz Be'eri, where more than 10 per cent of the population was murdered, including, as he described, an infant in her pyjamas, shot in the head. "How do I feel? Determined. Very determined," he said.

A desire for revenge is understandable. But Israel should be—needs to be—better than that. Hamas is a terrorist organization. Israel is a democratic state. And a full-scale invasion of Gaza will lead to horrific consequences, both humanitarian and geopolitical.

I'm obviously not a military strategist, but I am a human being. And I cannot see the benefit of bombing public infrastructure and apartment buildings, of forcing all those people out of their homes.

Yes, Hamas is known to embed their operations among citizens to use them as human shields.

But Israel knows this.

Yes, Israel warned citizens of Gaza to leave. But to do so on such short notice seems cruel. And where are they to go?

Perhaps that was Hamas's strategy all along: to inspire an Israeli response that the world would despise, with Gazans as human pawns. But pointing fingers at Hamas, as fair and accurate as this exercise might be, won't change the fact that Gazans are enduring a catastrophe. And while Israel has said it would not block humanitarian aid to Gaza from Egypt, so long as supplies don't reach Hamas, that won't come close to solving that crisis.

Yes, the actions of Hamas were horrific. Yes, Israel has the right to defend itself: to rescue those hostages, hunt down the perpetrators, shore up its defences. Yes, yes, yes. But how far will this go? Already the misery in Gaza is horrific: displaced families, women with crying babies, men hauling around mattresses, starving and thirsty people desperate for safety as bombs fall all around.

Never again, remember?

Whether they were supporters of Hamas or not, there is a danger that Gazans and other Palestinians will be motivated to support it. If Israel invades and occupies Gaza, it will only lead to more death, more strife, more hatred—and then how can we ever hope for peace?

I am absolutely not victim blaming: this is just a logical consequence of continued escalation.

Even some families of Israeli victims have called for restraint. "It seems to me that if in the worst days of their lives they can keep their humanity, the rest of us can follow their example," wrote Ami Dar, the Israeli-born founder of the NGO Idealist.org, on X.

For Jews, the establishment of a State of Israel wasn't just about hope. It was insurance, of "never again." And now, at the very time we need that insurance, hope has dissolved into fear.

There is so much to be afraid of—for people living in Israel, Gaza, the West Bank, and other Arab nations; for Jews everywhere, who have witnessed a modern-day pogrom, followed by some international celebration and atrocity denial. There is so much fear for people everywhere, knowing how far this could escalate.

OCTOBER 25TH, 2023

One day after an eighty-five-year-old released hostage
tells a news conference that she "went through hell"
during the just over two weeks she was held by Hamas.

On the night of October 8th, the day after the Hamas massacre that killed more than 1,400 people in Israel, I was woken in Vancouver by a knock on a door. *This is it,* I thought. *They've come for me.*

"They" were the Hamas terrorists, the latest version of the shadowy Jew-haters—Nazis, previously—that I have feared my whole life, as the child of Holocaust survivors. In recurring nightmares, but also in conscious moments, such as when I allow myself to contemplate what will happen if "never again" becomes "again"—another mass extinction event targeting Jews.

And on that night, Thanksgiving Sunday, roused from a fitful sleep, this was my first very real thought. (What was actually going on: my kid was having a birthday sleepover, and it was a friend knocking on his bedroom door.)

I know this imagination-leap sounds ridiculous. But as I wrote in my first book, *Kiss the Red Stairs*, about intergenerational trauma, this is where my brain goes, without fail. "Stressful event, Holocaust. Joyful event, Holocaust." It's visceral. But an event like an actual massacre of Jews—well, I had never experienced anything like it when I wrote those words.

For many people like me, these irrational fears were severely triggered by the events of October 7th. It wasn't just the largest number of Jews killed in a single day since the Holocaust—although that would be traumatizing enough—but the horrific way in which civilians, including children and babies, were murdered.

"When the mind was groping to find what this horribleness was like . . . very quickly there was a total connection with the Holocaust," Yael Danieli, the founder of the International Center for MultiGenerational Legacies of Trauma, told me this week by phone. "The connections are absolutely unmistakable. Fear for survival, fear of annihilation. The vulnerability, the helplessness."

Also triggering has been much of the response to the Hamas massacre of Jewish people: synagogues vandalized and, in Tunisia, burned down. In Toronto, pro-Palestinian protesters harassing patrons of a Jewish-owned restaurant. Around the world—in Vancouver, too—we saw people tearing down "Missing" posters meant to create awareness of the children who were abducted by Hamas.

This is not just repulsive. For some of us, it is terrifying. Our cellular memory has been activated by current events. The intergenerational trauma in our genes is raging.

French author Anne Berest describes her own intergenerational trauma in *The Postcard*, a literary sensation about her family's Holocaust history.

"I carry within me, inscribed in the very cells of my body, the memory of an experience of danger so violent that sometimes I think I really lived it myself, or that I'll be forced to relive it one day. To me, death always feels near. I have a sense of being hunted."

Yes, yes, exactly.

One person commented to me recently that this moment we are in feels like the early 1930s. That's a terrible thing for anyone to imagine. But for a Jewish person, it is beyond chilling.

The existential dread is exacerbated by what we're seeing around us. The antisemitic comments and atrocity denial, the open letters by students at Toronto Metropolitan University and other universities openly dismissing—and in many cases justifying—the barbarism committed by Hamas.

"It's what we call the trauma after the trauma," says Dr. Danieli, a clinical psychologist who works with Holocaust survivors and their children as well as other severely traumatized people around the world. "The judgmental indifference of the onlookers."

This response has been extremely triggering for people like me, who have spent years imagining what it would have been like had we been born near the beginning of the last century instead of closer to the end. And which of our non-Jewish friends would hide us if it did come to that.

The intergenerational trauma is also affecting Palestinians, who have dealt with displacement, oppression, and worse for decades—and, in Gaza, as they are being pummelled by Israeli air strikes. Gazans "feel as if their lives are this horrible movie that just gets rewound and started all over again," former CNN foreign correspondent Arwa Damon told NPR.

This war is not merely a triggering event for those of us already suffering. It is an inciting event for people today and future generations of Palestinians and Jews. "Forget everything you thought you knew or you learned about dealing with trauma, because this is different; this is an ongoing event," Israeli author and clinical psychologist Ayelet Gundar-Goshen told CNN.

So people like me are confronting another of our worst fears. After working to prevent our inherited trauma from migrating down into the next generation, we see that our children will be suffering from a new event, one that will be remembered—consciously and on the cellular level—long after our own nightmares have ceased.

OCTOBER 26TH, 2023

One day after Benjamin Netanyahu stated that Israel was
"raining down hellfire on Hamas" and had "eliminated
thousands of terrorists—and this is only the beginning."

The Irish band the Mary Wallopers played the Hollywood Theatre in Vancouver this week.

During the show, a band member said something about a free Palestine.

This, according to attendee Hanah Van Borek, led to a few shouts from the audience: "Fuck the Jews!"

It was clearly audible in her area of the crowd, a person who was with her confirms, but nobody around them shut this down. There were some cheers of support, though. "My whole body went into shock," says Ms. Van Borek, who is Jewish.

Ms. Van Borek left the venue and explained why to security staff. She says a worker encouraged her to go back inside and reassured her she was safe. "Nobody will be able to tell that you're Jewish," he said, according to Ms. Van Borek. (Oy.)

She did return to the show, but Ms. Van Borek was—and is—rattled. She supports the band's right to make political statements. It was the shouts from this group—and the silence around them—that were alarming.

A representative for the band told *The Globe and Mail* in a statement that they did not hear the antisemitic comment, and if they had, they would have confronted the culprit and had them ejected. They also released an Instagram statement saying their gigs should be a safe space.

Given the horrific massacre of civilians conducted by Hamas in Israel on October 7th, and the deadly response of the Israeli military in Gaza, it is not surprising that intense emotions associated with it are bleeding into the cultural landscape. This is what artists do: think about big ideas and massive crises—sometimes of the heart, sometimes geopolitical. Sometimes both.

It is not at all wrong for an artist to express their views onstage. A pro-Palestinian message onstage at a concert is absolutely fine. Hate speech and racial slurs are not.

Echoes of the war in the Middle East have reached the cultural world—music, publishing, visual arts, even comedy. The visual-art publication *Artforum* issued an open letter about the war that did not mention the October 7th massacre, angering many in that community, and leading to a second open letter signed by other artists condemning the first.

A storied New York literary series at 92NY cancelled a scheduled appearance by Pulitzer Prize–winning novelist Viet Thanh Nguyen. He had signed an open letter condemning Israel.

That last-minute cancellation resulted in other writers who had been booked for the series pulling out from future events in protest, including Canadian Dionne Brand. Some 92NY staff resigned in protest. And then 92NY cancelled the whole series for the rest of the season.

I understand that 92NY's roots (it was founded 150 years ago to serve the American Jewish community) may have informed this decision, but I don't understand not giving artists a platform to speak.

An award ceremony for Palestinian author Adania Shibli planned for the Frankfurt Book Fair last week was cancelled after the Hamas attacks. Her acclaimed novel is about the rape and murder of a Palestinian girl by Israeli soldiers in 1949, based on a true story.

This is the exact time we need to hear from the artists. I want to know what they are thinking.

Here in Canada, the novelist Jasmine Sealy, introducing a panel discussion at the Vancouver Writers Fest last week, said that because she had the microphone, she was going to use the opportunity to call for an end to the "violent occupation of Palestine."

Some audience members were very unhappy about what they saw as one-sided support and complained to the festival (which declined an interview request, as did Ms. Sealy).

Is it Ms. Sealy's right to say something? Of course. Was it her place, as moderator of a panel about female protagonists in fiction, to make an overtly political statement in her introduction? That's less clear to me. But when you are the artist in the spotlight, that spotlight is yours.

The war, with so many people in the diaspora strongly connected, has created or exacerbated divisions that have pitted artists against each other. Sometimes it gets personal—and ugly.

Debate is a keystone of cultural communities. But some of these divisions have gone beyond healthy dialogue.

As patrons—not just big-bucks philanthropists but on-the-ground buyers of tickets and books—we also have a say. To support or not to support. You can buy Ms. Shibli's novel. You can choose the store where you want to buy your next book.

As the statements—and sometimes the insults—fly, I hope to hear more, not less, from artists. And certainly there will be great art that comes out of this horrific time.

OCTOBER 31ST, 2023

*One day after Israel's ground assault into Gaza deepens. Three
days after actor Matthew Perry's death at the age of fifty-four.*

I haven't been sleeping very well lately. Maybe you can relate.

The war in the Middle East has been the primary culprit;
being a fifty-something woman hasn't helped.

I have been picking up my phone in the middle of the night,
doom scrolling like crazy, even while totally aware that this is not
doing any favours for my already teetering mental health.

I have an entire to-be-read system in my bedroom—shelves,
piles—but I can't even seem to focus on books, my forever
happy place. The need for distraction is intense; the phone is
my frenemy.

*You can pick it up as long as you don't read anything about the
war* is my 2 a.m. instruction to myself.

An impossible task. I can't just scroll past. I need to know.
Even if I don't necessarily want to know.

The war has been shattering for so many of us with close connections to people involved. For Jews like me, there has been the added horror of feeling targeted by a rising, acceptable, even celebrated antisemitism. It has been a horrible time.

So on these deepest, darkest nights, I've been putting down the phone and picking up my iPad instead. Looking for something light and funny to relax me and keep me company, I've been going nostalgic. You probably know where this is going, my friends.

For three weeks, on my worst nights, I had been rewatching *Friends*, in search of fairly mindless—but, in fact, very clever—entertainment to distract and lull me back to sleep. As a result, my fitful sleep has had the soundtrack of Chandler Bing et al. riffing and angsting about things that were a luxury to care about.

And then Matthew Perry died.

This would have been a blow at any time, but it feels particularly gutting now. I know, comparing a celebrity's before-his-time death to thousands of innocent civilians being killed in Israel and Gaza sounds ridiculous. And I'm not comparing. It's just that this character he embodied had become part of my coping strategy. Beyond that, I have felt personally invested in Mr. Perry's well-being.

Last year, I spent hours listening to Mr. Perry talk about his life.

He was candid, contemplative, self-aware, and hilarious in his memoir *Friends, Lovers, and the Big Terrible Thing*. Listening to the audiobook, as I did, made absorbing the story even more of an intimate experience. Mr. Perry was in my ears, talking about his Ottawa childhood and coming-of-age, the universe plot twist that allowed him to audition for the role of Chandler, the superstardom that resulted, and his years-long battle with addiction.

As the audiobook experience does, the narrator/author began to feel like more than that. He was a faraway friend, and I was rooting for him. Rewatching *Friends*, I hoped he had conquered his monsters.

This week I have gone from using the show as a distraction—no longer an option—to watching my favourite Chandler Bing episodes.

The one where he gets trapped in an ATM vestibule with Victoria's Secret model Jill Goodacre during a power outage. The one where his relationship with Monica is discovered. The one where he proposes to her.

Mr. Perry was a comedic genius. His perfect timing, his physical gestures, his invention of a way of speaking that has become part of the lexicon—yes, genius. Could he have *been* any funnier, any more influential? Now what had been an exercise in distraction has become part of my grieving process.

I wish I could end this on some sort of wise, bright, optimistic note. Optimism is in short supply these days, I'm afraid. But there is still wisdom.

Late Monday, the British Columbia government announced that Holocaust education would become mandatory for all high school students. One speaker at the event was survivor and esteemed psychiatrist Robert Krell.

Dr. Krell, who is very wise, was speaking about how bad things feel in the world right now. He addressed the rise of anti-semitism that has followed a massacre of Jewish people. This has been particularly horrific for Holocaust survivors to witness.

"On October 7th, Hamas brought Auschwitz to Israel. It slaughtered babies in front of their parents and vice versa, tortured and raped women, and burned alive entire families," he told the crowd.

Trying to offer some sort of encouraging message in the midst of all this, Dr. Krell cited the philosophy of Elie Wiesel—survivor of Auschwitz, author of *Night*, winner of the Nobel Peace Prize.

What Dr. Krell had heard Mr. Wiesel say on several occasions concerned Jewish people specifically, but in this dark moment, I hope Mr. Wiesel would be okay with extending this to humanity in general.

"We Jews have every reason to despair, but we cannot," Dr. Krell said. "We are commanded to hope."

One day after the White House announces that Israel has
agreed to pause attacks in Gaza for four hours a day. But the
incursion rages on, with thousands already killed.

I met a man named Faisal Salama at a pro-Palestinian rally in Vancouver. Mr. Salama, thirty, had just moved to the city. He is Palestinian—born in Kuwait, raised in Edmonton—and still has family in Gaza, including an aunt and first cousins, now displaced from the north as Israeli bombs rain down. His family was relocated to Gaza in 1948 when they lost their home in Ashdod, a city on the Mediterranean coast. Mr. Salama's father, who was seven at the time, still lives in Kuwait as a stateless refugee.

My heart was breaking, listening to his story. It was also pounding.

I had been asked to answer a question: Why are so many people, chiefly among the younger generations, so anti-Israel? How did this tiny country of less than ten million people go from darling of the left and beacon of democracy in the Middle East to being so utterly reviled—especially by progressives?

For instance, how much do you have to hate a country to actively seek out and tear down posters of its abducted children—often with glee?

I've seen the hostility myself on social media, where people argue about the details of the October 7th attacks (Were babies really beheaded?) and some even refuse to type "Israel" in full, replacing the middle vowels with asterisks, as if it's a swear word.[1] But I wanted to talk to some actual people. A pro-Palestinian protest seemed like the right place to do that.

I was nervous. I had seen demonstrations in other cities turn nasty—with some people inciting hatred against Israel and Jews. But this was a peaceful gathering of a few hundred people outside the Vancouver Art Gallery. There was an Indigenous blessing and a choir performed peace songs in the rain. The prevailing message was: Ceasefire now. Stop the assault on Gaza. Save the children.

Still, criticism of Israel was fierce.

"Israel is not a true country, a true state," said co-organizer Janine Solanki, who is with the group Mobilization Against War and Occupation. After the October 7th attacks, MAWO put out a statement celebrating what it called "defensive military operations"

---

[1] I later learned that this was being done to prevent being shadow-banned from social media sites. That said, there are plenty of instances where I see the country's name written as "Israel"—in quotation marks, or "so-called Israel," suggesting it is an illegitimate country.

by "Palestinian resistance fighters" and decrying "the Israeli Zionist propaganda machine and mainstream imperialist media" for "frantically trying to paint Israel as a victim of terrorism."

Ms. Solanki told the crowd, "We are the world, we are the majority, and we will win because we are on the side of humanity; we are on the right side."

The day before the rally, I had spoken with Malka Daniels, a business student at Toronto Metropolitan University, a campus she describes as hostile these days for Jewish students like herself. Since October 7th, Ms. Daniels, twenty-two, has heard other students call for an intifada and chant "by any means necessary."

When she took part in what was supposed to be a counter-demonstration by a handful of Jewish students, she says they were told to "go back to where you came from!" (Thornhill, in her case), and after being surrounded by what she estimates were dozens of protesters, the Jewish students had to be escorted away by TMU security. As they were leaving, a protester reportedly yelled, "It's too bad Hitler didn't finish the job."

I am not a person without skin in this horrible game. I grew up in a Jewish enclave of Toronto, where the slogan "Israel Is Real" was a common sight, and attended Hebrew school part-time. This is where I received my initial education about the State of Israel—a reverent narrative that, I realized much later, lacked any Palestinian perspective.

I had learned at home why Israel had been founded. My parents survived the Holocaust, and to them, Israel was a haven. Had it existed when they were young, their parents and siblings might have been able to escape Poland, might not have been murdered in gas chambers. My mother might have been in Tel Aviv at nineteen instead of in Auschwitz.

Tel Aviv is where I spent my own nineteenth birthday, during a summer working on a kibbutz. One of the first images I saw on October 7th was a giant cloud of rocket smoke rising from the city where that kibbutz is located.

This baggage brings with it a bias, many readers will point out. Fair. But I am also a human being, and a mother. And I feel sick watching the bombing of Gaza and the displacement of its people. Israel is going after Hamas, but civilians are suffering in horrific ways. It's not hard to see why people are critical of Israel.

The pro-Palestinian protest movement has been active for decades. But it has taken on new life. It had been "very much marginalized, because our society doesn't allow for criticism of Israel and doesn't allow for pro-Palestinian sentiments to be expressed without pretty significant consequences," says Roberta Lexier at Mount Royal University in Calgary, whose teaching focuses on social movements, social change, and leftist politics. "Something has changed for sure recently, and we're seeing it really play out on a large scale."

Dr. Lexier makes it clear that she does not support the actions of Hamas, but explains that "people today have a better understanding of that reaction to oppression. It's normal that people are going to fight back against their oppressors."

There have been pro-Palestinian demonstrations all over the world in the weeks since the October 7th attacks and the punishing response by the Israeli army. Protests have drawn tens of thousands of people. More are planned this weekend.

"People like me have come out of the closet," says Osgoode Hall Law School associate professor Faisal Bhabha, who condemned York University for its response to a statement by student unions describing the October 7th attacks as "a strong act of resistance" and referring to Israel as "so-called Israel." (York insisted the statement be retracted; Mr. Bhabha disagrees.) These days more people are looking at Israel through the eyes of the Global South, he says. "So you've got people who were not raised in the Eurocentric post–World War II era in which the Holocaust is this dominant frame for understanding inequality."

When Israel was established after the Second World War, there was great international sympathy for Jewish people, after the Holocaust. The Six-Day War in 1967, when Israel captured the West Bank and the Gaza Strip, may have been a turning point.

"I think there was a major shift post-1967, where prior to that, Israel was viewed as the David rather than the Goliath," says Tilly Shemer of the Shalom Hartman Institute, a Jewish-focused think tank operating in Israel and North America. Since "a lot of people in progressive circles want to simplify this conflict into who has power and who doesn't have power," she says, "that leads them to always side with Palestinians, and even Hamas, as the vulnerable party, and see this as black and white. They don't allow themselves to see this as grey or to see Israel as vulnerable." One glaring omission in this view from the West, she says, is the extent to which Israel feels under a constant threat of terrorism.

If there was a moment of international sympathy for Israel after the October 7th attacks (and that is a big if), it was almost immediately replaced by concerns about what Israel might do in retaliation.

Supporters of Israel wonder why it is so loudly vilified for its sins when other countries' evils are ignored. Where are the protests for the Uyghurs, the Rohingya, the two hundred thousand Afghan refugees recently forced to leave Pakistan? Why, the comedian and late-night host Bill Maher recently wondered, with all the other terrible regimes around the world, is Israel singled out with so much antipathy?

"Why this one place? Why does this arouse [so much hatred], especially among young people . . . who hated Trump because he wouldn't condemn the people with the tiki torches?" Mr. Maher said, citing the protesters who chanted "Jews will not replace us" at the infamous rally in Charlottesville, Virginia. Referring to young progressives, Mr. Maher said, "You're the ones with the tiki torches now."

There's a meme I've seen going around social media: "No Jews, no news." In other words: the reason Israel's actions come under such close scrutiny internationally has everything to do with it being the Jewish state; it's antisemitism. There is a feeling that people who hate Jews and/or Israel have been waiting for this moment, where they can freely express their disdain/hatred with impunity—even draw praise for it.

Hillel is an organization for Jewish post-secondary students around the world. Its largest chapter, Hillel Ontario, represents some fourteen thousand students at nine universities. Since October 7th, it has been contacted by a lot of them. "We've heard from students who say, 'I used to be friends with this person; this person is now calling me a murderer, a baby killer; someone who supports genocide,'" says Hillel Ontario's Jay Solomon. "These accusations are not simply levelled at people who are pro-Israel. It's people who are Jews."

I did not witness such conflation at the Vancouver event. Those I spoke to who were critical of Israel (i.e., everyone) were careful to clearly separate their condemnation of Israel from criticism of Jewish people.

"I feel that Jewish people around the world all deserve safety and deserve protection," Mahsa Shobbar, thirty-one, told me. "However, not at the expense of another group."

The word "genocide" was used frequently, though—in speeches, on signs, and in conversations I had with attendees. It is also ubiquitous on social media when referring to Israel's treatment of the Palestinians, its current assault against Gaza in particular.

The term was coined by Jewish lawyer and activist Raphael Lemkin[2] during the Holocaust to describe a conspiracy to exterminate a national, racial, or religious group. Historian Simon Sebag recently wrote in *The Atlantic* that no genocide has taken place, nor has it been intended. It is a tragedy, he wrote, but not a genocide. He went on to say that the word "genocide" has been so devalued that it has become meaningless.

The term being used indiscriminately is particularly triggering for supporters of Israel, a state formed as the result of genocide.

Critics of Israel also speak about white supremacy, settler-colonialism, and they call for land back to its Indigenous inhabitants. These protests have also been empowered with the rise of decolonization movements.

---

2 On December 29, 2023, the Lemkin Institute for Genocide Prevention and Human Security, a U.S.-based international non-profit organization, issued a statement declaring that Israel's actions against Gaza constitute genocide. In the same statement, it said that Hamas's October 7th attacks had genocidal dimensions. The institute has no connection to Lemkin himself. Prior to this statement being issued, members of the Lemkin family had said they were outraged that the institute would use Raphael Lemkin's name to pursue what they described as an extreme anti-Israel agenda. *The Times of Israel* responded to the Lemkin Institute's statement with an opinion piece accusing the Lemkin Institute of betraying its name. In response to this and other criticism, the Lemkin Institute released a statement saying it welcomes communication with the Lemkin family. "While we may disagree, we remain steadfast in our mission and in our support of Raphael Lemkin's legacy."

Even Mr. Salama, with his own Palestinian story, told me his views on Israel are heavily informed by his life in Canada as a settler on Indigenous land.

You will often hear Israel described as a colonial or imperialist entity and Israelis as settler-colonialists. And in this current environment where colonialism is reviled—for good reason—Israel is seen as one opportunity for a colonial construct to be dismantled. In this narrative, Israelis/Jews are seen as the colonizers and their power judged as white supremacy—even if Jews have existed there for thousands of years and many are not white. Israel's demise could be a triumph for decolonization efforts.

These are all alluring catchphrases that are easy to take to heart, digest, and spit out in solidarity. In this age of social media, they are highly effective. Even if they don't tell the whole story.

This war—and the protest against it—is not just taking place in the streets. From almost the moment Hamas launched its attacks, we've all been able to follow along.

But social media is also rife with misinformation, and users don't always have the skills to spot a Photoshop, misleading propaganda, or outright lies.

Ruby Dagher, an expert on the Middle East and conflict in general who currently teaches at the University of Ottawa, has seen incendiary and inaccurate social media posts. One said Israelis believe in the extermination of Arabs. "All of the discourses that are happening right now are approached in a way where it's either hatred or victimization, or just suffering."

The stories of suffering are ubiquitous. And now the world is watching this in real time.

"The Hamas attack was horrific. It was unjustifiable. It was all of those things. But [Israel's] response has been particularly disproportionate," Dr. Lexier says. "It's kind of collective punishment against a group of people." She says part of the prevailing anti-Israel sentiment comes from that. "We're bombing refugee camps because there's one guy we think is a terrorist in there, and who cares about all the civilians?"

Depending on where you stand, you could simply say: Israel is reviled because it does terrible things (particularly under the leadership of Prime Minister Benjamin Netanyahu).

Or on the other side of this ever-widening divide: People hate Israel because of antisemitism.

But nothing about this is simple—no matter what young progressives are being told by some activists.

"We have been lied to for years and years that the Israel–Palestine conflict is complicated," Ms. Solanki said at Saturday's rally, before referencing the "criminal Zionist project."

In fact, the issue is complex and far more nuanced than much of the current discourse would suggest. It is being simplified for all sorts of reasons—because of the limitations of social media; for ease; to make powerful points; because the people uttering these simplifications have an agenda themselves, or don't really understand. Perhaps because they are so justifiably upset that they aren't motivated to do a deep historical dive.

Because this is urgent. There are innocent children dying every day in Gaza.

And isn't that reason enough to hate Israel?

I should state that there are people who love Israel very much. They are being drowned out by an anti-Israel sentiment that is raging not just in the Palestinian territories—where that hatred is understandably entrenched—or the hostile Arab lands that surround it, but here, in the West. And in circles where many Jews, until just over a month ago, would have felt very much at home.

Jess Burke, who works for the Centre for Israel and Jewish Affairs (CIJA), says there is strong anti-Israel sentiment among young people and especially in progressive spaces, where she says there is an expectation that people identify as anti-Zionist. She describes it as an "if you're not for us, you're against us" kind of attitude.

Ms. Burke says the trope of Jewish people being powerful and in control—of media, government, the economy—is a factor. "People feel like they're punching up; it's virtuous. If you can dismantle the person who is the proverbial oppressor, you are on the side of goodness, you are on the side of virtue, you are on the side of what is right."

What's been particularly galling for Ms. Burke is where much of this criticism is coming from: "women's spaces, reproductive-justice spaces, queer spaces, and from university campuses, spaces of higher learning, of enlightenment."

———

At Yale University, Jewish student Sahar Tartak sat outside what she described as an anti-Israel event that drew hundreds of students and faculty. She was outside, she says, because she was barred from attending. What she heard through the door, according to her post on X: "Israel cannot remain the state of the Jewish people." That it "is trying to inflict as much harm, damage, and death as possible." She heard Hamas described as "a resistance group."

At a Vancouver rally last month, a Langara College English department instructor, Natalie Knight, praised the Hamas attacks, calling them "amazing, brilliant." She is now on leave.[3]

A disturbing video circulated this week of hostilities being spewed at Jewish students at Montreal's Concordia University.

It all makes one wonder just what young people are learning these days.

Today's students are generations removed from Holocaust survivors and veterans who fought in the Second World War. They did not grow up on the war stories recounted to baby boomers and Gen Xers, even millennials—or the lessons that came with those stories.

"I think the average kid sees it as old European history," says Dara Solomon, executive director of the Toronto Holocaust Museum. "So if that's the case, they probably do not understand that the formation of the State of Israel was because we needed a

---

[3] Natalie Knight was dismissed from Langara in January 2024.

homeland because our people had been decimated. I don't think they make the connection."

If the Holocaust has made criticizing Israel challenging—or even unseemly—in the past, it's becoming less of a factor as those events move further into history.

Ms. Burke at CIJA was conducting a training session for a city council group, including mayoral staff, in Ontario (she would not disclose the municipality) on October 27th about antisemitism—not Israel. While discussing the Holocaust, Ms. Burke says, she was told by an attendee, "I cannot sit here and listen to the story that Jews are innocent and that Jews are oppressed." That person left the meeting.

"I do believe that there is a before and an after that October 7th marks that we didn't necessarily sign up for—but that will be a part of our reality for many, many generations to come," Ms. Burke says.

Both Ontario and British Columbia have announced changes around Holocaust education—in B.C., making it mandatory for all high school students, and in Ontario, expanding the already mandatory Holocaust curriculum. At both announcements, the rise in antisemitism after the Hamas attacks was mentioned.

These efforts are welcome, but they may be too late for this moment.

"I think people have really taken their stances, and I don't think people's unconscious bias will allow them to productively see another side to an issue," says Ms. Daniels, the TMU student.

"It seems as though education might be a little too late to catch up to the backlash."

The acrimony and violence seem to be escalating, including overnight shootings of two Montreal Jewish schools this week.

The Vancouver rally was peaceful. There were no placards suggesting Zionists belong in garbage cans, like I've seen at other pro-Palestinian marches. I saw no one shouting at the guy quietly holding his "God=Love/Hamas=Hate" sign.

But there is so much hate right now, everywhere. And I don't know how we come back from this. Or where we go.

NOVEMBER 16TH, 2023

*The body of a nineteen-year-old Israeli hostage is recovered
near Gaza's largest hospital. The previous day,
Israeli forces had entered the hospital, which it
said was used by Hamas militants.
Gaza health authorities announce this week
that the death toll had exceeded twelve thousand people.*

The award ceremony for the Scotiabank Giller Prize, Canada's leading literary prize for fiction, was interrupted—twice—this week. During the live broadcast, protesters shouted anti-Israel slogans and held up signs accusing the award's title sponsor, Scotiabank, of being complicit in genocide as a result of its investment in an Israeli arms manufacturer.

Three people in their twenties faced charges of obstructing, interrupting, and interfering with the lawful use, enjoyment, or operation of property, and use of a forged document. Toronto

Police allege the demonstrators used fake or doctored credentials to get into the event, identifying themselves as event crew, media, or guests.

Protesters also shouted at Prime Minister Justin Trudeau this week at a Vancouver restaurant. When he moved on to a different establishment, the police sent one hundred officers to the scene as a large protest formed outside. Two people were arrested—one for allegedly assaulting an officer, the other for obstruction.

These incidents have generated a lot of discussion about when and where protest is appropriate. Is it okay to mar one of the rare occasions when Canadian writers are celebrated in grand style? Is it okay to throw a wrench into the prime minister's social evening?

Protest is a cornerstone of any democracy and should be not only allowed but encouraged. That said, it doesn't belong everywhere—courts have set out that the right to free assembly does not include the right to physically impede or blockade lawful activities. But there are certainly more urgent examples than those two where protest should be considered offside, as war in the Middle East rages.

Protests, for instance, do not belong outside a Jewish-owned restaurant, as happened at Café Landwer in Toronto. Or on the windows of a Jewish-owned bookstore—Indigo—especially on the anniversary of Kristallnacht, when German pogroms targeted Jewish businesses, homes, and synagogues.

Protests do not belong outside synagogues and mosques.

Protests of course belong on university campuses, but not when they are intimidating or threatening. Universities have an obligation to allow for protest, but even more importantly, to ensure the safety of their students. Jewish students do not feel safe at many Canadian universities right now—and back home, their parents are freaking out.

In Toronto, pro-Palestinian protests have been held outside Chrystia Freeland's constituency office. Fine. Except some crossed the street to face a Jewish community centre, which houses a daycare and schools.

Antisemitism has infiltrated some of these demonstrations. If the protesters are not concerned with how this makes their Jewish fellow citizens feel, they should know that it delegitimizes the message.

At a Vancouver protest, the former head of the BC Civil Liberties Association, Harsha Walia, said, "How beautiful is the spirit to get free that Palestinians literally learned how to fly on hang gliders."[1] Consider what those paragliding people did after they landed on October 7th: murdered, raped, and abducted innocent civilians attending a concert in the desert.

Incendiary language of any type is dangerous. Online white supremacist rhetoric has clearly led to deadly consequences,

---

[1] According to reports, including in *The National Post* and *The Toronto Sun.*

including the murders of the Afzaals, a Muslim family, in London, Ontario.[2]

Yelling "Heil Hitler" at people holding a rally for Israel in Washington, D.C., is not okay. Nor is throwing money at Jewish city council members, as protesters did in Berkeley, California, this week.

Mr. Trudeau trying to enjoy a dinner out? Fair game. He's the prime minister.

Targeting the biggest night in Canadian literature took the shine off the event; some people left, no longer comfortable being there. But comfort is a lot less urgent than babies dying in Gaza. When things are dire, decorum can of course fall away.

Besides, isn't it a writer's prerogative—obligation, even—to speak out?

At the National Book Awards this week, a group of writers, in a coordinated move, took the stage and called for a ceasefire in Gaza. It was meaningful and impactful.

---

[2] In June 2021, a young man who had been radicalized online against Muslims rammed his truck into five members of a Pakistani-Canadian family who were out for a walk in London, Ontario. Four of them were killed: Salman Afzaal and Madiha Salman, both in their forties; their fifteen-year-old daughter, Yumnah Afzaal; and her paternal grandmother, Talat Afzaal, seventy-four. A nine-year-old boy was injured but survived. On February 22nd, 2024, a judge ruled that the attack was an act of terrorism and sentenced the attacker to life in prison.

Many Canadian writers believe the Giller protest was appropriate. Many have signed an open letter in support of the protesters, urging that the charges against them be dropped. They include this year's winner, Sarah Bernstein, as well as previous winners Omar El Akkad and Sean Michaels.

The letter would have been stronger had it not led with the protest specifically, but the real matter at hand, which it does eventually get to: it urges a ceasefire, condemns the Israeli government, and calls for an end to the "75-year occupation of Palestine."

I do wonder where this kind of support from artistic quarters was for Israeli hostages (who did earn a brief mention in this week's letter) and around 1,200 murdered people, including babies and children. Instead, after October 7th, there was deafening silence—or, even worse, justification.

Justifying murder is never okay. Neither is racism, or making kids feel unsafe.

But protest is powerful. And we need artists' voices. Let's hear them, from all sides.

POSTSCRIPT: *Five people were ultimately charged in connection with the Giller protest. In December, 2024, the pro-Palestinian group CanLit Responds announced that charges against four of the five protesters had been withdrawn.*

For Kelly Baron, now ex-publisher of the Canadian literary journal *The Ex-Puritan*, the final straw was a statement reposted by a colleague on Instagram. It accused Israelis of stealing Palestinian bodies for their skin due to allegedly high rates of skin cancer for Israelis—the suggestion being that Jews are not indigenous to the region.

Even before the skin-stealing post, Ms. Baron felt, after the Hamas attacks on Israel and the subsequent war in Gaza by Israel, that some social media activity by CanLit colleagues went beyond support for Palestinians and strayed into antisemitic territory.

"There was no outcry on October 7th. I signed onto social media and saw that my peers and colleagues were either celebrating it or rationalizing it as an act of resistance," says Ms. Baron, who is Jewish. She says she originally gave the Toronto-based magazine six months' working notice but resigned effective immediately on Monday.

The skin-cancer allegation was a post too far. It cited a Gaza spokesperson who said, "'Israel' [in quotation marks] steals our Martyrs' bodies." And in a second post: "they occupy us, steal our dead bodies, & wear our skin."

It was reposted by a colleague at the journal on his personal account, who in another post, referred to "so-called Israel." He also shared a statement from another account claiming "Israel admits burning hundreds of people on 7 October."

"This is so far removed from Palestinian liberation. I don't know how anyone can think this is effective for any kind of social movement," says Ms. Baron, who shared screenshots with me.

(A similar claim was recently made by model Gigi Hadid; advocates for Israel have slammed these allegations as repeating the ancient blood libel against Jews.)

Skin-stealing aside, Ms. Baron's former colleague is certainly not alone in CanLit circles in describing Israel as a so-called nation.

An open letter following the disruption of the Scotiabank Giller Prize ceremony calls for charges to be dropped against the protesters and for Israel to end the "75-year occupation" of Palestine, which questions the legitimacy of Israel's existence. It asks for the release of "all hostages"—equating the Israelis taken hostage by Hamas with Palestinians held in Israeli jails.

The letter shares deep concerns about the catastrophic suffering of Palestinian civilians at the hands of Israel. But it only mentions the October 7th attacks in relation to the Canadian condemnation they attracted, without condemning them directly. And it makes no mention of the horrific sexual assaults of Israeli women by the Hamas attackers.

At the very least, this feels like a troubling oversight.

I don't know who specifically wrote the letter of support for the Giller Prize protesters; when I asked the first signatory, Canadian author Farzana Doctor, she said she was one of many who collaborated on it. "We worked as a collective," she told me by email.

Another open letter has been written in response by Canadian authors Sidura Ludwig and Anna Rosner. It says the first Giller letter was disturbing and distressing in that it shared alienating biases and contained glaring omissions. Hamas was not mentioned at all, it points out, and it says citing a "75-year occupation" without acknowledging over three thousand years of Jewish presence in the land "erases the Jewish narrative from the current conflict."

The letter states that "incomplete narratives spark the growing hatred against Jews and result in further Jewish isolation during a time when communities seeking peace must come together."

Each letter has more than two thousand signatures.

There are so many open letters going around that it can be hard to keep track, but the one that led to the dismissal of the head of the University of Alberta Sexual Assault Centre was particularly egregious in that it called the sexual assaults of Israeli women an "unverified accusation." This letter, since taken down, was signed by academics as well as politicians Sarah Jama, an Ontario MPP, and Susan Kim, a Victoria city councillor.

After much outcry, Ms. Kim removed her signature. But when Victoria's mayor was asked by reporters whether she believed people were raped during the Hamas attack, Marianne Alto said, "I don't have enough information to be able to answer that in an informed way."[1]

The silence from people who have espoused the #BelieveWomen mantra is loud and hurtful. There's a meme going around: "#MeToo unless you're a Jew."

Open letters may be performative, but they are also of value. People who are justifiably angry and anguished feel compelled to do something, say something. Writers and other artists especially feel the need to voice their views. But if a letter dismisses the value of human lives on either side—or calls into question (or ignores) sexual assault, please think about what you're signing. Or posting.

---

[1] According to news reports, including in the *Victoria Times Colonist* and CHEK News.

One day after fighting resumes following the temporary
ceasefire that allowed for a hostage–prisoner exchange.

As the first group of Israeli hostages was being released from Gaza
on Friday, a new Palestinian/Israeli restaurant was preparing for
its first evening of business in Vancouver.

Bar Haifa is owned by a group of friends, Palestinian and
Jewish. A larger, more upscale offshoot of their Toronto establishment the Haifa Room, this downtown Vancouver spot was
supposed to open months ago, but the universe (and construc-
tion delays) had other plans.

Its opening night ended up taking place just shy of seven
weeks into the war.

"We questioned if we should open at all," Mark Kupfert told
me, as five of the six partners sat around a table the day before
the airy restaurant's official opening. "It just seemed wrong
and off. And then we discussed that maybe it's actually more

important because there's all this heartbreaking, devastating news every day. Like this story is maybe what's needed."

It has been so hard to find any hope for so many of us who have connections to the Middle East over these past weeks. I thought maybe I could find some at this new restaurant, with this amazing ownership structure: descendants of Palestinian refugees and Holocaust survivors opening a restaurant together.

Mr. Kupfert's grandparents were Holocaust survivors who came to Canada after the Second World War; his grandfather's brother immigrated to Palestine. He was born and raised in Montreal.

Waseem Dabdoub's grandparents were displaced from their home in Akko, in what is now Israel, and became refugees in Lebanon. He was born and raised in Windsor, Ontario.

Fadi Hakim's father is Palestinian from Haifa. He had to leave the country for Lebanon, where he met Mr. Hakim's mother. Mr. Hakim was born and raised in Toronto.

Joseph (Yossi) Misrahi Eastwood was born to Jewish parents in a Jerusalem bomb shelter just before the 1967 Six-Day War. His mother had escaped from Nazi occupation in Greece. His father's family's roots in Jerusalem go back at least six generations. The family moved to Toronto when he was three.

Friendship and food across the divide; what could be more healing? Pollyannaish, I know.

As the echoes of this war reverberate through the world, causing ugly divides, even food has become an issue.

At a pro-Palestinian rally in Vancouver last month, one person I spoke to described what they called the renaming of Palestinian dishes as a form of genocide. Israeli salad, for instance.

There is a sort of Yelp protest going on as well, as keyboard warriors give one-star reviews to Palestinian or Israeli restaurants, depending on which side of the issue they are on. "Every one-star review from Zionists is a badge of honour to us," the Vancouver restaurant Tamam posted on its Instagram page.

When Bar Haifa announced it was opening, there was a lot of love, but also some angry reaction, Mr. Kupfert says. Comments such as "you'd better not be serving Israeli wine."

Like its ownership structure, Bar Haifa is all about fusion food. "There's this age-old thing," says Mr. Hakim. "Who's got the better hummus? Who's got the better falafel?"

For the falafel, they discussed family recipes, traditions, and preferences, each offering strong opinions ("It's supposed to look like the desert inside," Mr. Misrahi Eastwood argued).

"We tried it thirty-six different ways. And we had a spreadsheet," says Mr. Hakim. "It came together organically, with a lot of fighting and a lot of Coca-Cola just to cut the grease."

They don't all agree about politics either. "We have differences of opinion on the matter; it's so personal," Mr. Dabdoub says.

"But there is this ability to communicate and sit down and see each other's humanity no matter what," Mr. Kupfert says.

"When you have to work together, it's very, very, very important that all other opinions are respected. And in that you . . .

distill all of that down," says Mr. Hakim. "Just like we did with our falafel."

I can report that the collaborative hummus and pita are out of this world. (I didn't get to try the falafel.[1]) But the most nourishing part of that afternoon for me was the chat.

No meal, no matter how delicious, can solve a crisis of such magnitude, obviously. Nor can a cross-the-divide joint venture. But breaking bread in a place like this can feel very good. And feeling good is in very short supply these days. And maybe that's good enough, for an evening at least.

---

[1] I can now report that the falafel is also out of this world.

*Three days after Calgary mayor Jyoti Gondek announces she
will not attend the city's thirty-fifth annual menorah lighting
ceremony, saying the event had become too political. Two days
after U.S. secretary of state Antony Blinken publicly criticizes
Israel for not protecting civilian lives in Gaza.*

The festive season is upon us. Perhaps your weekends are jammed
with opportunities for holiday gaiety. Parties, parades, performances, shopping. Eating.

All the stuff that brings light and warmth when the darkness
descends so early, the nights are at their longest, and are also
very cold.

Normally, I eat all this holiday merriment up, along with every
shortbread cookie that falls within two metres of my grasp.

Things feel different this year.

I'm not sure about you, but I am finding it challenging to
fully indulge in the festive vibe. It's hard to get into the holiday

spirit when innocent civilians who don't have the good fortune of living in Canada are being bombed or held hostage. When we are being pummelled with terrible news from the Middle East, as well as the seemingly endless war in Ukraine; the cost of living, homelessness, and deadly drug crisis on the home front; and a climate catastrophe everywhere.

I know, it was ever thus: global and domestic trouble that we manage to ignore while we stuff our stockings, and ourselves, with holiday goodies.

Perhaps it feels particularly absurd to celebrate in the midst of the brutal Israel–Hamas war because it is constantly in the headlines. Or because many of us have personal connections to that part of the world and to people who are personally affected. The horrific Islamophobia and antisemitism that have arisen over here as a result are not doing much to fuel the holiday spirit.

I wrapped my son's first Hanukkah gift on Wednesday night and turned on the radio. CBC's *As It Happens* was interviewing an Israeli, Shai Wenkert, whose twenty-two-year-old son Omer has been held hostage by Hamas since October 7th[1]. Immediately, the act of wrapping a light-up Frisbee felt obscene.

So much of this feels wrong. Wrapping gifts—even with the dregs of festive paper that I have extracted from the corners of various closets—seems ridiculous as the planet burns/floods/

---

[1] Omer Wenkert was released on February 22, 2025, after more than 500 days in captivity.

deteriorates. Then there's all the hostility; I have read more open letters than holiday cards this year.

The absolute privilege of having the opportunity to attend an office gathering or participate in a Secret Santa swap feels discomfiting. This festive season, I don't feel like jingle-belling even half the way.

Who could have imagined during the lost COVID Christmases of 2020 and 2021 that there would be a time when it would feel safe to gather with others but it didn't feel particularly appealing, didn't feel exactly right?

Let me add another issue to the mix: fear. Canadian Jews who are celebrating Hanukkah this weekend have been flooding Facebook groups with discussions about whether it's safe to put a menorah in the window this year, as is tradition. Jews are also debating taking down the mezuzahs (rectangular cases containing a small parchment prayer scroll wrapped inside) from their doorposts, worried that these instantly identify the home as a place where Jews live. Seeing a video last weekend of a verbal antisemitic attack on Vancouver public transit didn't help my own anxiety.

Then my fifteen-year-old son said to me, "I think we should skip the Hanukkah lights this year." It's not the hydro bill he's worried about.

Still, I am putting that menorah in the window. And I am certainly not removing my mezuzah. I might, however, skip the giant lawn dreidel this year. (It's a pain to inflate, anyway.)

Pre-COVID, I held a big annual Hanukkah bash, filling my

tiny house with friends, latkes, wine. This year, with just about two months to go before the holiday, I started working on a celebratory "save the date" notice announcing the post-pandemic return of the party. That was on October 6th. I never sent it out.

Ultimately, I decided I do want—need, actually—to gather with people, especially family and those who have reached out during what has obviously been a difficult time. There will be latkes; there will be wine (oh, there will be wine). But I am imagining more of a warm community gathering than a lampshades-on-heads situation.

So I haven't gone full-on Grinch. Not yet.

The holidays can be so hard. Geopolitics aside, many people are suffering personal grief. The near constant bombardment of yuletide cheer from every direction can be painful. Even a trip to the grocery store can be triggering.

So here's a wish for your Christmas, Hanukkah, Kwanzaa, whatever you celebrate (or don't): that you are able to be with people who make you feel safe and good. That you can do things that make you feel good. (Giant holiday crossword? Hell, yeah.) That you can get a break from whatever it is that is causing you stress or distress.

My real wish feels impossible: peace on Earth. But perhaps we can at least try for goodwill toward each other.

PART TWO

The Time Before

~

Cries of anguish from long ago.

October 7th did not start on October 7, 2023. The history behind the attacks and the war that followed could fill volumes. I can't offer that depth here, but I wanted to provide some context with a brief history about the Israel/Palestine conflict, before sharing some pieces that I wrote before that catastrophic year.

This is in no way comprehensive, but I hope this summary is helpful.

The Zionism movement began in the late nineteenth century by Jews in Europe who had been terrorized by persecution, including discriminatory laws and deadly pogroms, especially in Eastern Europe and Russia.

In 1896, Theodor Herzl, a Jewish Hungarian-born lawyer and writer who is now known as the father of Zionism, published a pamphlet calling for "a restoration of the Jewish state."

The goal was to get Jewish people away from the killing, raping and pillaging; the dream was self-determination. Safety, liberation and independence. But where to go?

Palestine.

The movement ultimately set its sights on the ancient and ancestral home of the Jewish people, going back some three thousand years. It was a land in the Middle East from which they had been largely, but not completely, exiled historically. The term "Zionism" comes from a biblical Hebrew word for Jerusalem: *Tziyon*, or Zion.

(When interviewing someone at the pro-Palestinian rally for the piece in the previous section that ran in November, 2023, I asked her about the indigeneity of Jewish people on that land. She replied with a question of her own about where I had received this information. *The bible?* she asked. Well, yeah. But also historical and archaeological evidence.)

This land that the Zionists wanted to settle was not sitting there empty, waiting for them. It was already home to many people—mostly Arabs, who formed the majority, as well as a Jewish minority (and others).

In 1917, the Zionist dream—and Palestinian nightmare—moved closer to reality with the issuing of the Balfour Declaration. It was a letter from British foreign secretary Arthur Balfour that stated, in part: "His Majesty's Government view with favour the establishment in Palestine of a national home for the Jewish people, and will use their best endeavours to facilitate the achievement of this object, it being clearly understood that nothing shall be done which may prejudice the civil and religious rights of existing non-Jewish communities in Palestine or the rights and political status enjoyed by Jews in any other country."

After the First World War and the defeat of the Ottoman Empire, the League of Nations put Britain in charge of the land.

It became known as Mandatory Palestine. The land experienced large-scale Jewish immigration, primarily from Eastern Europe and the Soviet Union.

The Zionism movement gained worldwide (although not unanimous) sympathy and support after the horrors inflicted on the Jews during the Second World War became known. The Holocaust killed two out of every three European Jews. As of 2024, the worldwide Jewish population had still not recovered to pre-Holocaust levels. It wasn't just the murders committed by the Germans that were so catastrophic, but the door-closing committed by the rest of the world, ensuring there would be no escape for the Jews. Few countries, including Canada and the U.S., were willing to accept Jewish refugees in adequate numbers—or at all.

After the war, the world saw that Jews needed a safe land of their own, although many countries didn't want to take in the Jews themselves. Many Holocaust survivors had already chosen Palestine as their new home, not always with permission from Britain.

In 1947, the United Nations approved a partition plan for Palestine: The land, still under British control at the time, would be divided between a Jewish state and an Arab state. Jerusalem would become an international city.

The plan would have given more land to the Jews—who were still a minority—than the Arab majority, and it would have caused a mass migration of Arabs (the term "Palestinian" did not come into common widespread use until later). So, as in

Partition between India and Pakistan, it was an imperfect plan. But it was a two-state solution.

Arab countries rejected the proposal. Britain left anyway, withdrawing officially at the end of May 14, 1948. That same day, a few hours earlier, without approval by Arab states representing the majority population of the land, Jewish leaders went ahead and declared the land the State of Israel. On May 15, the armies of five Arab nations—Lebanon, Syria, Jordan, Egypt and Iraq—attacked.

Israel, defying expectations, won what became known as The War of Independence, capturing more of the disputed land than they would have received under the UN plan. Egypt took the Gaza Strip and Jordan the West Bank.

These events are known by Palestinians as the Nakba—the catastrophe. And it was catastrophic. About 700,000 to 750,000 Arabs were expelled from or fled their homes under extreme duress. Many were forced out by Israel, including by Jewish militias before the war began. These were often violent expulsions. (An expulsion in and of itself is a form of violence.) Others, it is said, left under instructions by Arab leaders— again, war was coming or already waging—with promises that they would be able to return. (This is a disputed narrative.) Hundreds of Palestinian villages were destroyed. Some "decided" to leave to avoid war or expulsion—not exactly a decision made with agency.

Decades later, they have not been allowed to return. And 750,000 refugees have become about 6 million, living in the West

Bank, Gaza, Jordan, Syria and Lebanon. Refugee status is passed down through generations.

UNRWA (the United Nations Relief and Works Agency for Palestine Refugees in the Near East) was created to deal with the displaced Palestinians. The agency was meant to be a temporary solution to the humanitarian crisis. It is still operating.

About 150,000 Arabs remained in Israel after the war and are known by some as Israeli Arabs or Palestinian Israelis. Today, they make up just over 20 per cent of the population of Israel proper. Most are citizens; those living in Jerusalem are still primarily considered "permanent residents."

In the years following Israel's independence, about 850,000 Jews were expelled from Muslim-majority countries or, experiencing extreme antisemitism, left of their own accord. Many of these Sephardic and Mizrahi Jews from Algeria, Egypt, Iraq, Libya, Morocco, Tunisia and Yemen migrated to the new nation of Israel.

In Israel, conscription was introduced. All Israelis—male and female—must do service in the Israeli Defense Forces, the IDF. Exceptions are made for non-Druze and non-Circassian Arab Israelis, who do not serve. Ultra-Orthodox Jews are also exempt, although this is the subject of much division within Israel and may be slowly changing. Some people refuse for ideological reasons; they do not want to serve in the military and they perform social service work instead. This number is growing.

In 1956, Israel aided Britain and France in invading Egypt in an attempt to take back control of the Suez Canal.

Then, in 1967, came the war that changed the boundaries—and history. What is known as the Six Day War began when Israel, expecting an attack by Egypt and Syria, struck first. Israel captured the Golan Heights, in the north, from Syria; the West Bank and East Jerusalem from Jordan; and, in the south, the Sinai Peninsula and Gaza from Egypt.

(The West Bank is called Judea and Samaria, the biblical name of the region, by the Israeli government, as well as some Israelis and supporters of Israel.)

After this war, Israel annexed East Jerusalem, including the Old City, where the Western Wall and Temple Mount, the holiest site in Judaism, are located. This is where the Al Aqsa Mosque, the third-holiest site in Islam, also stands. Israel also annexed the Golan Heights.

Palestinians in the West Bank, Gaza and East Jerusalem came under Israel's control.

There were more wars. The surprise Yom Kippur attack on Israel in 1973 and conflicts with Lebanon and Gaza, ultimately leading to the events of October 7th, 2023. But I'm getting ahead of myself here.

In 1978, Israel and Egypt signed the Camp David Accords, leading to a peace treaty the following year that saw the Sinai returned to Egypt. Egypt acknowledged Israel, a huge, historical moment, which earned Israeli Prime Minister Menachem Begin and Egyptian President Anwar Sadat the Nobel Peace Prize. It also cost Sadat his life. He was assassinated by the Egyptian Islamic Jihad in 1981.

In 1994, Jordan and Israel also made peace.

Throughout all of this, there were points when peace felt possible. Picture the image of Palestine Liberation Organization leader Yasser Arafat shaking hands with Israeli Prime Minister Yitzhak Rabin, as then-U.S. President Bill Clinton smiles between them, his arms outstretched. This was in 1993, the signing of the first Oslo Accord, which would have seen Palestinian self-governance in the West Bank and Gaza, eventually leading to a Palestinian state. A second accord, signed in 1995, went into more detail on the land-for-peace agreement.

But peace was not to be. In 1995, Rabin was assassinated by a far-right Jewish extremist opposed to the agreements. The following year, Benjamin Netanyahu—who was opposed to the Oslo Accords— was elected. And things deteriorated from there. Talks broke down in 2000; Ehud Barak was Israeli prime minister by then, with Arafat still negotiating for the Palestinians.

(Again, let me emphasize, this is just a summary.)

The First Intifada, or the Shaking Off, was a Palestinian uprising that began in 1987. Palestinians fought their Israeli oppressors by throwing stones and Molotov cocktails, primarily in the West Bank.

The Second Intifada, sparked by a purposely provocative visit in 2000 by then-opposition leader Ariel Sharon to the Temple Mount and fueled by the failure to make progress toward Palestinian self-rule, was much more intense, and deadly. Palestinian suicide bombers killed Israeli citizens on buses, in restaurants, and other crowded public areas. Israel responded with its own deadly force. The reported number of deaths varies, but more than 1000 Israelis were killed and as many as 5000 Palestinians.

In 2002, Israel began building the security wall—or separation wall—around the West Bank. Life became much more difficult for Palestinians, as the barrier sliced through communities and farmland and impeded freedom of movement. It also became safer for Israelis, with suicide bombings cut significantly.

In 2005, Israel withdrew from Gaza, which it had occupied since 1967. The occupation was over, as was the Second Intifada, but Israel controlled the shared borders, airspace and shoreline on the Mediterranean Sea.

In 2006, Palestinians elected a Hamas government in Gaza. Hamas, whose founding charter calls for Jihad and the elimination of Israel, proceeded to remove its Palestinian rivals from Gaza. In response, Israel and Egypt imposed a blockade, limiting movement of people and goods in and out of Gaza.

There have been no more elections. Hamas, considered a terrorist organization by Canada and the U.S., has remained in power since, and was in power when it launched the October 7th, 2023 attacks.

The West Bank remains under Israeli occupation. While Palestinians live miserable lives under tight rule, Israel allows the building of settlements for Jews. Israeli settlers are not always motivated by ideology—some large, especially Orthodox, families are after a less expensive place to live—but many are. And their treatment of their Palestinian neighbours has often been racist, ruthless and violent. The IDF does little to prevent this violence or protect the Palestinians living there.

Netanyahu has rejected a two-state solution and allowed the expansion of these settlements, which are considered illegal under international law. Israelis who oppose a Palestinian state often cite safety as their primary concern.

A two-state solution—which I and many others desperately hope for—would see an independent state in the West Bank and Gaza. It would exist alongside Israel. There would be peace. Or, at least, an end to this deadly conflict.

This, I hope, gives some sense of how we got here: catastrophe upon catastrophe, leading to only more. I encourage further reading on this subject—and reading from all "sides" of the issue.

In putting together this collection, I read through my *Globe and Mail* archive, searching for stories that dealt with issues relating to Jewish culture, including my own identity. When I conducted this exercise, I was surprised, although I guess I shouldn't have been, by the sadness. So much tragedy. So many stories touched on the Holocaust or the ongoing conflict in Israel/Palestine. We've included just a few of them—again, published here as they were written originally, with a few notes and, in rare cases, minor alterations to correct copy errors (and in one case, to paraphrase text quoted from another publication that I did not receive permission to use here).

APRIL 1998

As I read through my itinerary, a chill runs through me.

Monday: Cemetery, Ghetto. Tuesday: Orphanage. Wednesday: Treblinka. Thursday: Auschwitz.

I am going home.

I suppose Poland isn't really my home, or even the home of my parents, despite the fact they were both born there. But the things that happened in these terrible places, the things that happened to my parents, who somehow survived, and my grandparents, who did not—these things happened at "home." And these things are my horrifying heritage; they define me.

Sadly, my mother called Thursday's destination "home" for three harrowing months, although I'm sure that word never actually escaped her chapped and thirsty lips to describe her prison, Auschwitz.

So why do I venture back to this land that was so hostile to my people, to my parents? Why go back to look at piles of hair and ashes, at ominous blackened chimneys, at blossoming fields that conceal immense cemeteries?

These are questions I ask myself as I prepare to travel to Poland, along with my mother, two sisters, and my niece, and many other survivors, children of survivors, and grandchildren. We will participate in what's called the March of the Living. Thousands of Jews from around the world will march along the railway tracks from Auschwitz to Birkenau on Yom HaShoah, the day to commemorate the Holocaust. We will carry Israeli flags and sing "Hatikvah," the Jewish[1] national anthem (meaning "hope"), on the killing fields that claimed our parents and grandparents. We will say Kaddish for these people, the prayer for the dead. We will recite this prayer for millions of dead people—children, mothers, fathers, husbands, wives, aunts, uncles, grandparents. My grandparents.

It sounds almost romantic, this group of Jews gathering to assert our existence and to thumb our collective noses at the Nazis. It sounds cathartic, an appropriate end for a piece of tragic literature. But this is not fiction. And I suspect the ending cannot be happy, no matter how triumphant we may seem as we march along those tracks that took our ancestors to their deaths.

There will be a sense of closure, I suspect. And a sense of victory. You killed my grandparents. You tried to kill my

---

[1] "Hatikvah" is actually the Israeli national anthem, not the "Jewish" national anthem. Many years after I wrote this, I find it interesting that I conflated the two.

parents. You tried to extinguish my people. But now I am back. And I will not let the story of your killing die. I will tell anyone who will listen. I will force those who will not listen to learn the dreadful truth.

Am I wrong to return with my mother? My sisters and I agonize over this question. As a teenager, my mother had the strength to somehow survive numerous labour and concentration camps, even the notorious Auschwitz. But will she survive this trip back to hell intact? When she enters through the gates of the camp and sees the infamous words "*Arbeit Macht Frei*" (work will set you free) once again, what turmoil will she go through?

Will she show us the barracks she slept in, the piece of flat wood that gave her a few hours of rest each night? Will she point and say, "There—that's where I was beaten by a soldier for mumbling my name at roll call"? Will she pose for a photograph in the room where her head was shaved?

Some Holocaust survivors and children of survivors refuse to set foot on German or Polish soil. They don't want to benefit the economy of a country like Poland, where Jewish groups who pay homage to the dead are still taunted by youths shouting "*Heil Hitler*." Others simply can't bear the pain.

Before his death, my father ventured back to Poland, where he was born, and Germany, where he survived the war under a false identity. Imprisoned in a labour camp in Poland,[2] he managed to

---

[2] I understand now that it was not a labour camp, but a ghetto, where he was a forced labourer.

secure false papers and escape to Germany. Jacob Lederman, Polish Jew, became Tadek Rudnicki, Polish Catholic. For two and a half years, he laboured on a farm six days a week, eating—no, devouring—bacon and pork when it was available, celebrating Easter, praying to Jesus. Each Sunday he would lead the family to church, urging them to hurry, not to be late.

Once inside, with the wafer of communion in his mouth, my father quietly called forth his own God, urging Him to end the war, to keep him safe, to keep his family safe. For two and a half years, my father prayed that no one would see him go to the bathroom. God did end the war, and He did keep my father safe. But not a single member of my father's immediate family survived. His parents, older sister, and little brother all died in the gas chamber.

When my father returned to Germany in 1979, he received a hero's welcome from the farming family with whom he lived during the war. There were celebrations, large (porkless) meals, gifts, and warm hugs.

But when he ventured to Poland, it was a much more difficult experience. He visited Treblinka, where his parents, brother, and sister were gassed. "I walked around the death camp for a few hours," he wrote in his journal, "trying to figure out the layout and operation there. The ramp is intact, so are some roads built by Jewish slaves. . . . It is so quiet and green everywhere—so different from those horrible times!"

He visited his childhood home: "I am in the room where I left my family, never to see them again. It is a shattering experience. I am breaking up and can't talk any more. Extremely heartbroken."

The woman who lived there remembered my father's parents. She told him they had left a letter for him, but after more than thirty years without word, she had thrown it away, figuring my father had died in the war. This was devastating information.

Upon visiting a cemetery[3], my father wrote, "I found all mass graves, took some pictures of that tragic scene, looked with horror at that huge grave which my dear, gentle brother with sweat and blood over his face helped to dig under the inhuman rigour of the SS."

My father was in Lodz, the city of his birth, for the High Holidays. The few Jews left spent the morning in synagogue, then invited my father home for a Rosh Hashanah meal. They served ham.

My father came back from that trip early. He could not stand to be in the land of his persecution any longer. He wanted to hold his wife, his children.

I tell people I am looking forward to my heritage trip, but the truth is I have never been so scared of anything in my life. Am I crazy for going? Is this my way of paying homage to the grandparents I never knew? What exactly am I trying to prove here?

I am going to prove my existence. I am going to spit on the demonic plans of Hitler, simply by walking on land he tried to make *Judenfrei* (free of Jews) with gas and guns. I am going. And, if nothing else, I simply *am*. I exist. I breathe.

---

[3] This is not actually a cemetery, but a forest where Jews were murdered en masse.

During his trip back to the killing fields, my father wrote, "I am realizing the great obligation attached to me, the last one of all my family. . . . I won't forget you, my dear restless souls gliding over the greenery of Treblinka."

With this trip, I am fulfilling my obligation. I am refusing to forget.

When he was a young boy in Germany, Fred Herzog—back then he was Ulrich; the name Fred came later, in Canada— remembers his mother showing him her school picture, pointing to the Jewish girls in the photo. They were the smartest in the class, she told her young son. Even as a child, he could sense her resentment.

This memory has stayed with Herzog the way a photograph holds on to a moment. It's there, always, even if it remains tucked away in a drawer.

Photographs would, eventually, become a refuge for Herzog. The boy who saw too much in wartime found some peace behind a camera, training his sights on his adopted city of Vancouver with the eager eye of a new arrival, and the skill of a master. For decades, he took tens of thousands of Kodachrome slides that sat largely unseen. It wasn't until he was well into his seventies that recognition came—for his photographs, which burst with colour and history, and for himself, a pioneer in his craft.

Fred Herzog had risen from the ashes of his bombed-out youth in Germany to illuminate the history of Vancouver, as arguably the city's most important—if, for many years, obscure—visual documentarian.

But even a hundred thousand images of the new world cannot erase the traumas of the past.

Last fall, I had occasion to interview Herzog, who is eighty-one, at his modest home on the west side of Vancouver. The book *Fred Herzog: Photographs* was being published, and it was an opportunity to talk about his life, his method, the impact of his late-in-life success.

Our conversation about art derailed into what he later described to me as a collision. The turn came when Herzog offered his thoughts on the Holocaust—or, as he initially referred to it, "the so-called Holocaust."

It was a conversation that has stayed with me for months as I returned to Herzog for subsequent discussions, the story was considered by my editors, and I struggled with its meaning and with its potential impact on how Herzog's career will be assessed.

There was—there is—a personal struggle, too. I am a child of Holocaust survivors.

All He Owned, Gone.
Ulrich Herzog was born in the German town of Bad Friedrichshall in 1930 and grew up in Stuttgart amid the intensifying hold of the

Nazis. His father was deeply concerned; he knew no good could come of war. His mother, however, was more supportive of the Nazi campaign, even taking young Ulrich to one of Hitler's rallies in 1938.

There was no glory in wartime. His mother died in 1941, after contracting paratyphoid. His father survived his factory being bombed—he was home eating lunch. In 1944, the family home, too, was bombed. Nobody was hurt—Ulrich was safely in the nearby town of Rottweil—but it was devastating. "This was the biggest trauma I personally suffered," Herzog told me. "All my books and toys and things I owned were gone."

His sister's boyfriend, a Hitler Youth leader whom the artist remembers as a fine person and a good role model, was drafted into the army at eighteen and died within days of arriving in Russia.

Six months after the war ended—a humiliating defeat for Germany—Herzog was back in school.

"One of the most surprising and devastating things to me was meeting after the war was over with my schoolmates, and not one of them would talk about their war experiences," he said. "They only wanted to talk about soccer. That was devastating to me. I just could not believe that this war had already been forgotten by them."

His father died in 1946; Herzog feels the war and its trauma were responsible. Still in high school, Herzog was left in the care of an unloving stepmother who kept food from the children. Later, he worked for wealthy relatives who treated him poorly.

In 1952, Herzog left Germany for Canada, starting out in Toronto. He didn't have much but had brought his camera and other photographic equipment. Before the end of his first day in Toronto, Herzog was out of money. He sold his coin collection for a little less than four dollars and hocked his enlarger at a second-hand store.

That night—this was during a heat wave—Herzog was sitting on the porch of his rooming house, where the windows had been painted shut, when he met a neighbour, a medical photographer from South Africa. The meeting with this man would change Herzog's life. They found a basement suite to share and built a darkroom.

The following year, Herzog left for Vancouver. He worked on the ships in the port, where he earned the nickname Fritz—which became Fred. Eventually, he began working at the University of British Columbia as a medical photographer, taking his now-renowned street photographs on the side.

Vancouver Was His Muse

Herzog estimates he has taken about a hundred thousand colour photographs. (There are thirty thousand black-and-white images, too.) They represent a priceless record of a city whose subsequent growth has to a great extent wiped out the place he first encountered. They were also artistically pioneering; he was shooting in colour at a time when serious art photography was all about black and white.

It would not be unfair to call Herzog's images beautiful, yet they capture the less-than-pretty aspects of his adopted city. He chose to document the disenfranchised world of what is now Vancouver's Downtown Eastside rather than the ocean and the mountains; the squalor rather than the cherry blossoms; the working-class reality rather than the tourist-brochure fantasy. His photos are often populated with the downtrodden, the marginalized, the forgotten, and members of minority communities that were more invisible than visible at the time.

Herzog's work is powerfully honest: he often shot from the hip so as not to jar his subjects out of their candid moments. "When people see you, the picture's gone for good," he says. "You cannot repeat it. Once people have noticed you, you have to give up. That's it. You blew it."

For years, these works sat in the basement of Herzog's home. There were some private slide shows and he participated in the odd exhibition, but for the most part, his photos remained unseen.

With advances in technology, Herzog found a way to print his slides to his satisfaction (he insisted the prints match Kodachrome rather than real colours), a gallery to represent him—Andy Sylvester's Equinox Gallery—and widespread recognition with an exhibition at the Vancouver Art Gallery in 2007.

The retrospective, says Sylvester, was a turning point. "It allowed audiences to see . . . a substantial body of colour photography that started in 1953 and continues, that predates a lot of conventions in the history of . . . serious colour photography. I'm not talking about Vancouver. I'm talking about the world."

Unlike the masters of what has been called the Vancouver School—such as Jeff Wall, Rodney Graham, and Stan Douglas—Herzog's oeuvre is not photo-conceptual. Still, his name was being uttered in the same breath as theirs: here was a new master to celebrate, an overnight sensation who had been at it for half a century. At seventy-six, Herzog had found acclaim.

More exhibitions followed: There was a 2010 retrospective in Berlin; then, last year, a show at the National Gallery of Canada and Toronto's Museum of Contemporary Canadian Art. An ambitious retrospective—the inaugural exhibition at Equinox's new Project Space—was held over twice, with hundreds of people flocking on weekends to the East Vancouver warehouse space to see his photos.

He is on this year's shortlist for the fifty-thousand-dollar Scotiabank Photography Award, to be awarded Wednesday. And *Fred Herzog: Photographs*—with essays by Wall and Douglas Coupland, among others—is up for two BC Book Prizes, which will also be announced next week.[1]

"It's a phenomenon that in my thirty-one years I've never seen anything like," says Sylvester. "Because usually it takes decades. But it's also unusual to have a body of work sitting downstairs that he stubbornly stuck to. . . . Think about being a

---

[1] Fred Herzog did not win any of these prizes.

writer and constantly writing and no one's published your work for fifty-four years. I mean, you'd quit, right?"

The Collision

Fred Herzog's living room tells the story of his life: Its second-hand furniture is a testament to the many years of thrift-shop and garage-sale living necessary to support his photography. The Jack Shadbolt painting hanging over the couch is a now-achievable extravagance, thanks to his late-blooming career.

I was there on a rainy Friday morning in October for our interview, greeted with coffee and cookies served by Herzog's wife, Christel. I arrived a devoted fan; at one point, I had calculated whether I could possibly afford to buy one of Herzog's prints. (I concluded I could not.)

It's a question about his early time in Toronto that leads to the Holocaust. We're about thirty minutes into our conversation when I ask whether he, as a German, experienced any racism in postwar Toronto; I note that his employer—an importer of glass and china—was Jewish.

Herzog explains that George Zimmer, with whom he got along very well, had had a business in East Prussia before the war, a big furniture business, and that he must have sold it at a comparatively low price, given the times.

"He never complained to me about that," said Herzog. "That marks him as an unusual person, because even now, many of the people I know, many doctors, are Jewish. And there isn't one who spares me hearing about relatives who were, you know, treated badly during the war and the so-called Holocaust."

My throat goes tight.

"The business with the Germans rounding up the Jews and putting them into cattle cars is true, there's no doubt about that," he continued. "But there were other factors why there were so many undernourished people in the end, because the low-flying fighter bombers made it impossible to supply these camps with food, so there were many people very emaciated from not eating."

"You think that's because they couldn't get food supplies?" I ask.

"You couldn't," he says, and continues to explain.

I'm still having trouble believing where the conversation has gone and try to clarify what he is saying. "So do you believe," I ask, "that the Nazis would have fed the Jews better in these camps had the Allies not been bombing the area?"

He says he wishes he knew all the facts, but this is what he has read.

I had been mostly silent since the "so-called Holocaust" remark; my recorder captures the odd "uh huh" interspersed with his remarks. Finally, about five minutes after he said it, I return to the phrase. "You used the term 'so-called Holocaust.' Why did you?"

Herzog, who has a tendency to ramble, is stopped by my question. He starts to answer, stumbles over his words, takes a moment, then launches in.

"The Holocaust, I should perhaps not say 'so-called.' Here's what it is: I have, I'm interested [in] what went on, but I don't see how statistics were made or arrived at. The number of six million apparently was decided at a meeting in New York in 1945 or '46. And so I don't know whether it was six million or not. And here's what I say: If something is that awful . . . you don't have to exaggerate it. That there was a principle[2] injustice, and [that it was] indefensible by any standards—that, I have no trouble about. But that people were in such numbers gassed and gotten rid of—that is disputed, depending on where you come from. I don't dispute it, because I have a relative in Germany who used to be the personnel manager of the city where I come from, and he says he has seen the evidence, that he's seen the hardware that was used to gas people.

"But there were other books I have read which say much of this was actually delousing. The rooms with the gas were actually delousing rooms, because lice were one of the biggest problems and the biggest killers of Jews in the camps. So it's something I'd like to see a little bit more carefully, you know, collected: evidence and how the numbers are arrived [at]. That people were needlessly killed, there's no doubt. That people died on trains being transported is fact. That people died of hunger at the end of the war is fact. But many people, nine million Germans, were thrown out of wherever they lived. Nine million, and with no place to go. And many of those died of hunger and whatnot."

---

[2] I now wonder if the word should have been "principal." Either works in this context.

He pauses. Is my tape recorder running, he wants to know. Yes, I tell him. He seems troubled.

"It's personal," he says. "And I'm not against anything that is being said except that I would like to see it better documented."

Herzog is very clear that the Nazis "were absolutely mean toward Gypsies and Jews in a totally mean and stupid way," and that he did not like Hitler. "I have no love affair with the fascists. But I'm trying to find out the cause. I'm interested in facts." He points out that his wife's best friend, and his best friends, are Jewish. "So we're not against Jews," he says.

Christel Herzog, likely overhearing the conversation, drifts into the living room and sits, quietly listening. She seems concerned.

("I thought this was going to be about art," she would say to me later. So had I.)

With little prompting, even as we move on to continue the discussion of Herzog's career, and I ask how his late-in-life success has affected him, he returns to the subject of the Holocaust.

"I cannot convincingly say I think everything about it was the way it's being described. That's why I say 'so-called,' and I should not have said that. But what it says, there are some doubts in my mind that the real story is being told. And that is augmented by what happens between Israel and Palestine. The same lack of justice that the Jews experienced in Germany is now experienced by Palestinians in what used to be their country."

At the end of the interview, I reveal my own history to Herzog.

"I have to tell you about my family," I say. "My parents are

Holocaust survivors. My mother was in Auschwitz . . . and all my grandparents were murdered in gas chambers."

Taken aback, it is Herzog who now begins to ask the questions. "Even those who worked were never well-fed?" he wants to know.

"I stand corrected. I stand corrected," he finally says, and goes searching in his basement for a book of photographs by Roman Vishniac, whose pre-war pictures of Jews in Poland constitute an important archive. He insists I take it home. At the door, he is offering explanations; he tells me about his mother and that class photograph. He emphasizes that he seeks statistics in any matter; that he is in search of the truth, always.

I am shaking when I leave the house. Herzog's cozy living room on the west side of Vancouver is a million miles, a million years, from the horrors of the Second World War. And yet there they were, right in front of us: A wall. A bridge. Fred Herzog and I share a history.

The Holocaust

My father was born in Lodz, Poland, in 1919; my mother in Radom, Poland, in 1925. They were Jewish. Both are now dead, but throughout their lives they spoke often about the war.

My mother remembered well the German invasion of Poland in September 1939: it meant she couldn't return to school, after looking forward to it all summer. In 1941, her family was forced out of their comfortable apartment and moved into the cramped ghetto. Her little brother, who did not look Jewish, snuck out of the ghetto regularly, selling cigarettes in exchange for food. It was around this time that my mother was approached on the street by a German soldier and told to report to work cleaning barracks. Ironically, it was a lifesaver: From there, she became a forced labourer at a munitions factory and was there, working, when her parents and little brother were rounded up and deported to Treblinka. They were gassed on August 18th, 1942.

In 1944, my mother was sent to Auschwitz, where she was miraculously reunited with her sister. After more than two months of eluding what seemed a certain death, my mother was sent to a munitions factory in Lippstadt, Germany—a subcamp of Buchenwald. On March 29th, 1945, the inmates began a forced death march toward Bergen-Belsen. On April 1st, they were liberated by American soldiers.

My father escaped an execution-style death in either the Piotrkow Trybunalski or the Lodz ghetto (he was in both, and that is one detail I am unsure of)[3] by bribing a German soldier with a watch and promising to return with more jewellery. Instead, he ran, hid in a park, and ultimately managed to get false papers; the wife of a Polish official took pity on my father and his blue, blue eyes.

After the German defeat, my father went searching for his sister, asking freed Jewish women if they knew of her. That's how he met my mother. They married, had a daughter—classified as

---

[3] I now know for certain that he escaped from the Piotrkow ghetto; he was never, in fact, in the Lodz ghetto, despite being from Lodz.

a Displaced Person—and arrived in Canada in 1951. In Toronto, they had two more daughters. We never had grandparents.

"I Know That It Happened"

A few days after our interview, I call Herzog. It is not a conversation I'm looking forward to, but I need to speak to him again. Our talk ranges widely, shifting from the past to contemporary subjects such as the environment.

"I'm more focused actually on what's happening now," he says. "I have people who are very educated who say even if we did the right thing now, mankind cannot be saved. I just want to state that to you because it has to do with an orientation that's forward-orientated rather than backward-looking. So if I haven't fully understood the injustices of the Holocaust, it was probably because I just didn't want to read about it. I've seen the pictures and I know that it happened, but I did not research it and attach guilt to myself."

What about those books, I ask him, the ones with those delousing theories? How did he come to read them?

There was one book published in Switzerland, he says, a gift years ago from a house painter, now dead. "It presented a different view, which I know now is incorrect."

He says what he's been hearing about the Holocaust—from Jewish friends, including his ophthalmologist—is having an impact. "It's gradually been sinking in that this actually happened the way it's being described. But I'm the kind of person who, as I told you, would like to see how the numbers and the statistics were arrived at."

He says our discussion affected him. "You changed my point of view, to some extent."

Was it the trauma of living through the war at such a young age that had led to such a point of view?

"What has shaped me is growing up without parents who love me, more than anything else," he says. "That was what made me streetwise. Almost nothing else, not even the war, did that."

Months Later, Reconnection

Fred Herzog spent some time in Costa Rica this year, taking photographs. He returned in April, and I was able to talk with him yet again, after thinking about what he'd said for some time. Over the telephone, he repeatedly apologized.

"I have thought about the conversation a fair amount," he said. "I think the main thing, I was just unprepared for that question at that time. I was so overloaded with other issues that I could not have a level appreciation of your question."

I do not remind him that my question was simply whether he had experienced racism as a German in postwar Toronto. Also, I'm not looking for apologies. I believe he is sorry about what he said. What I want to know is why he said it.

"I was in a state of shock," he says. "When you brought it up, I reached into something that I no longer believe."

What did he once believe and where did that belief come from?

"The reason I gave you the wrong answer to the Holocaust. . . . To begin with, when I grew up in Germany after the war, nobody ever talked about the Holocaust. Nobody. Not my boss, not the other employees. Nobody there ever talked about the Holocaust. It was actually a seamless denial. And it was only after I had left Germany, I think there were some trials in West Germany where the Holocaust problem was driven home to Germans in such a way that they could no longer ignore it. . . . I remember reading right after the war that there were six million Jews killed, and I talked to people about that and most people said they had no idea. And I think, on the other hand, some people must have had an idea that bad things were happening but simply put their head in the sand."

We discuss a couple of his works: one of my favourites, *Black Man Pender*—a dignified Black gentleman holding the hand of his young daughter as they stroll through Vancouver's Chinatown with their cocker spaniel—and one of his, *Paris Café*. "The man in that picture looks somewhat disengaged, but I like the Santa Clauses and I like the price list of food," he says. "The whole atmosphere is somewhat in contradiction with the high-flying name 'Paris Café.' And I like that kind of inherent contradiction in many of my pictures. Every picture, I've sometimes said, has a curveball in it. They're not just pictures of pretty scenes. They're pictures that have a curveball in them which makes you think."

A Whirl of Contradictions

The curveball Fred Herzog threw in his living room last fall has left me shaken. What to make of these comments from the man who captured so sensitively and unblinkingly the underbelly of Vancouver?

They also, to stay with baseball metaphors, appear to have come out of left field. I have not been able to find any record of him saying such things before or since. Andy Sylvester, who has known him for years, has never heard any such thoughts. I spoke with Sarah Milroy, former *Globe and Mail* art critic, about this as well. As his biographical essayist for the new book, she spent many hours interviewing him, and he never expressed any such views, although they probed his war years deeply.

I did wonder about his state of mind at eighty-one, but listening to the interview, I am struck by his ability to remember small details and recount them with precision. He seems lucid and articulate. He suffers from some serious health problems, to be sure, but they do not appear to have been a factor here. During our last conversation, he told me, "My memory is not intact, and when my blood sugar is low, I quite often say nonsense. That wasn't the case when you talked to me and that incident occurred."

Cultural history is rife with debate about whether an artist's life or personal views matter to their work. Do Picasso's nudes look different when seen through the lens of his misogyny? Is it possible to listen to Wagner, to read Ezra Pound, without their antisemitic beliefs darkening the experience? Herzog doesn't belong in this company, but the question weighs on me: Should his art be reassessed in light of what he has said?

Walking through the Equinox Project Space, not quite five months after our meeting, I am a whirl of contradictions.

I look at the people around me, enraptured by the photographs and the memories they evoke. I wonder what they would think if they had heard the words I had heard. "So-called Holocaust."

Does the art look different to me? Yes, it does. But like the photographs, this is not black and white. In a way, the pictures look more interesting, more layered—rich with history: not only Vancouver's but the world's.

After months of living with this, I'm surprised: I am able, I think, to see it all through Herzog's battered lens.

I see his photography as the expression of a victim whose pain was not deemed valid in light of the atrocities of his countrymen and what others suffered; a young man who came to Canada and had to remain silent, but whose work speaks volumes.

I spend a lot of time in front of *Man with Cane*. An older Asian man—Chinese, probably—and a child stand by the stairs to the Ho Sun Hing Co. printing shop. I wonder what brought them there. Not to the grimy Chinatown sidewalk, but to Canada. Was it their own distress? Their parents'? Their ancestors'? Was it the hope of something better for their children? Whatever it was, it's no doubt a familiar story. It's what brought Fred Herzog here, my parents, so many of us. The man with the cane, too—who might be Irish or Ukrainian or who knows what.

What we have all escaped might differ in detail and scale, but here we all are: a grand collision.

POSTSCRIPT: *Fred Herzog died in 2019, predeceased by Christel in 2013.*

Post-graduation, theatre artists Joel Bernbaum and Kayvon Kelly were looking to explore young male friendship—and, frankly, drum up some work for themselves—when they began writing a play together six years ago. Of course, they had no way of knowing the work—which became a query on the sustainability of a Muslim-Jewish friendship—would have its world premiere at a time of war in Gaza and Israel.[1] Or that this premiere would take place at the 2014 Edinburgh Festival Fringe, where protesters would shut down a production from Israel.

Suddenly, their literal make-work project, their spiritual buddy play, took on an enormous topical resonance.

"Boy, we would never wish this to happen, but our play becomes even more important now and the responsibility

---

[1] This is a reference to the deadly Israel-Gaza conflict during July and August of 2014.

increases," says Mr. Bernbaum, co-creator of *My Rabbi*. "When I'm speaking those words on stage, it's a palpable taste in my mouth that this is so pertinent and so real right now."

In *My Rabbi*, Arya (Mr. Kelly) and Jacob (Mr. Bernbaum) are lifelong pals in Saskatoon. The death of Arya's father sends both on quests that bring them closer to their religions. Jacob, realizing his capacity for helping others as Arya grieves, becomes a rabbi. Arya travels to Iran to get in touch with his roots. Years later, they figure they can pick up the friendship where they left off. But it is not that simple.

The characters are loosely based on the co-creators, who grew up in Saskatoon but met at the Canadian College of Performing Arts in Victoria. Mr. Kelly, twenty-nine, is half-Iranian, the child of a Catholic mother and Muslim father. (He chose to be baptized Catholic at nine, but is now non-practising.) Mr. Bernbaum, thirty-three, has a Jewish father and converted to Judaism before his bar mitzvah.[2]

Shortly after graduation in 2008, they were in Vancouver to see a friend perform in *The Producers*. Over a pre-show pitcher of beer, they talked career plans. "We were thinking, well, we're not in the show; what do we do? Maybe we'd better write something," Mr. Kelly says over coffee in Vancouver, where he lives.

"So we grabbed a napkin and a pen, and we sketched out the first scene breakdown for *My Rabbi*," Mr. Bernbaum explains by phone from Saskatoon.

---

[2] In Judaism, religion is determined matrilineally.

"At first, we thought, oh well, maybe we just have a really funny comedy here," Mr. Kelly says. "You know, a really big Jewish guy and a little Muslim. But then we started thinking about how [for] so many people, those differences are actually the core of a problem versus the core of a great connection." So they threw in a hypothetical: "What happens if it starts to become a problem for us? What would it look like?"

It took six years to develop the show, and along the way, about two years ago, Mr. Kelly wondered if it was still relevant; the conflict had largely disappeared from the headlines, at least over here.

And then came the war between Israel and Hamas.

"I'm glad we're telling our story when we are because this is the time to encourage dialogue," Mr. Kelly says. "This is a time when we need to encourage bringing communities together to ask them to listen to each other. So for that [reason], I'm maybe glad it took us six years to get here because . . . we've arrived when maybe it's needed a little more."

The play had its world premiere at the Edinburgh Fringe in an uneasy atmosphere. Shows by an Israeli theatre group that received some Israeli government funds were cancelled by the venue after a noisy demonstration outside.

"I think it was a gross mistake . . . to concede to those groups," says Mr. Kelly, arguing that those who cancel a play (which was not political—it was described as a "darkly comic hip-hop fable") over concerns about the government funding it would also have to look at funding from other governments, such as the United States. "So I think it was a big mistake. Everyone was really on edge."

A palpable charge was in the air at the performances of *My Rabbi*, according to its co-creators. One group of young Muslim men was visibly upset by the arguments made by the Jacob character and then seemed to calm down as Arya countered them. "Their feelings on the issues were right on their sleeves," Mr. Kelly says.

It would be Pollyannaish to think art can fix the problems of the world—especially an ongoing situation of this depth and complexity. *My Rabbi* does not presume to offer answers, but its co-creators believe it is important to ask questions—and start a dialogue with Jews and Muslims (and others) together in a room.

"Art has both the ability and the responsibility to play a role in a situation like this," Mr. Bernbaum says. "And therefore it comes with an ethical responsibility to reflect the world in a way that engages people so that responsibility is passed on to the audience . . . [so] they feel that they're now responsible for showing up to this global situation. We are all participants. We are all responsible. And doing nothing is not acceptable. Saying nothing, asking no questions, that's not acceptable."

Martin Amis's excruciating and masterful new Auschwitz novel *The Zone of Interest* imagines what life would have been like on the administrative fringes of the concentration camp, for the people who ran the murder factory with precision and gusto, and the families who lived there with them. The horror unfolds from the perspective of three characters: Paul Doll is the buffoon of a commandant who lives with his wife, Hannah, and their children, and is busy climbing the concentration camp corporate ladder while dealing with the stress of increased transports (as if he didn't have enough on his plate, he complains). The "desk murderer" Angelus "Golo" Thomsen is a well-connected Nazi bureaucrat (a fictional character whose uncle is Martin Bormann, the real-life personal secretary to Adolf Hitler). And Szmul is a member of the Sonderkommando—Jews tasked with disposing the bodies of their fellow Jews after they were gassed—but not before extracting valuables such as their gold fillings. These were "the saddest men in the history of the world," Amis writes.

It is not the first time Amis—the larger-than-life bestselling British author of fourteen novels, two short story collections, and six works of non-fiction—has tackled the subject of the Holocaust. His 1991 novel *Time's Arrow* is also set partially at Auschwitz, in a tale told in reverse, so a doctor living in retirement in the U.S. goes backward in time eventually to the concentration camp, where people are plucked from the gas chamber, put on trains, and sent home to their families.

But Amis's experience writing *The Zone of Interest* was heightened, with much more at stake personally. The book is dedicated, in part, to the "countless significant Jews and quarter-Jews and half-Jews" in his life, in particular his mother-in-law, his younger daughters, and his wife.

"That was the difference between writing the first novel and writing the second," he explains in a telephone interview. "I've been with my wife for twenty years, and the children, our two girls, are seventeen and fifteen. So it was qualitatively different writing about it when your flesh and blood is involved. And of course my mother-in-law's family [from Hungary] suffered, as every Jewish family did. So I took it more personally. When I wrote the first book, I knew I couldn't do anything about the experience of the victims, and in this one I felt I could a bit. That I somehow had the right of entry into that experience that I didn't have before."

The book begins with Thomsen falling in love at first sight with Hannah. She is in a white dress and cream-coloured straw hat, laughing, encircled by her children, moving past the windmill, the maypole, the three-wheeled gallows ...

That was the scene that was in Amis's head, he explained in the interview from his Brooklyn home, when he sat down to write the book. "And then as often happens in the sort of magical way, all the rest just appeared."

The spark for the novel came when Amis learned in detail about the SS men bringing their families with them to live at the concentration camp. "I think it's an incredible fact that in fact the commandant at Auschwitz had his five children there. And I just thought they must have had a sort of simulacrum of a kind of social life. They must have played along as if there was some reasonable social dimension to what they were doing. And that had always sort of bothered me."

Amis has read deeply on the subject over these many years. "I never stopped reading about it," he says. "And I haven't stopped now. I've read several books about Hitler and Nazism since finishing the book."

The Zone of Interest has been described as a comedy set at Auschwitz and an office comedy—a description Amis "hated." Neither of these comes remotely close to describing the book. And for Amis, they rankled. He wanted to use humour not to get laughs but to illustrate the utter baseness, stupidity, vulgarity of the Nazi project.

"I wanted the irony to be militant, satirical, but I wouldn't call it a satire and I wouldn't call it a comedy. I'd call it a serious historical novel but [one] that does use mockery as well as revulsion." Hitler is never named in the book. (Amis employed a similar technique in his Soviet gulag novel *House of Meetings*, where Stalin's name is mentioned only once, in a footnote.) But after the last, devastating page, Amis has inserted a creepy photograph of Hitler with Bormann standing behind him, smiling like a smitten schoolgirl.

"My wife questioned it," Amis says. "But I thought it was Hitler looking so loutish and Bormann smiling juicily over his shoulder, I just thought it was evocative."

Amis, sixty-five, is a highly marketable author, and early reviews were glowing. (In Britain both *The Observer* and *The Spectator* called it the best thing he has written since *London Fields*, twenty-five years ago.) But his publishers in Germany and France passed on this book, leading to speculation that there may have been some discomfort about the subject matter given the Second World War history of those countries.

Amis's reaction? "As you'd expect, sort of all stunned and bitter." He says there was no conversation with his French publisher, and he received a "perfunctory" letter from his German publisher saying they'd found Thomsen's position unconvincing. (He has since secured a new publisher in France.)

"What you actually feel when that happens is that you thought you had a relationship with the publishers and in fact you don't.

I always assume that publishers go by whether they're going to do well with the book. So that's what I suspect they thought; that it wasn't going to do well. I'm reluctant to attribute anything grander to them than that."

Amis, who describes himself as a philosemite, believes anti-semitism continues to be an issue in Europe. "I promise you that when you bring up Israel anywhere in Europe [when public speaking], the whole atmosphere of the room changes," he says. "And there's no other explanation for it other than subconscious antisemitism. Nothing else explains it."

The situation in Israel might. Amis has always sympathized with Israel, he says, even if the country makes it "very hard for one to support it." He adds: "The Holocaust and Zion is one story. It's hard to separate the two historical streams. That's a symbol of renewal. Saul Bellow said to me that without Israel, Jewish manhood would have been finished. And there would have been nothing left for the Jews but abject assimilation and just forget the whole four-thousand-year story. And just hunker down and assimilate, become invisible. And that, as we know, hasn't happened."

Amis is now working on an autobiographical novel in which Bellow, along with Philip Larkin and Christopher Hitchens, are the main characters.[1] "This is really a response to Christopher's death in a way, because suddenly his story is over. It's complete. And I can write about him with a freedom that I didn't have, couldn't have had, couldn't have imagined while he was alive."

---

[1] *Inside Story* was published in 2020, Martin Amis's last novel.

Amis dedicates *The Zone of Interest* in part to two other deceased writers, Holocaust survivors Primo Levi and Paul Celan. In his acknowledgments, he shares a famous and powerful passage from Levi. Shortly after arriving at Auschwitz, packed into a shed with other prisoners and nursing a four-day thirst, Levi spotted an icicle through the window, reached out, and broke the icicle off—only to have a guard snatch it away from him. "Why?" Levi asked. The guard responded: *There is no why here.*

When looking for that impossible why, there's a sort of safety in thinking of the men (and women) who carried out these horrific crimes—and manufactured the mechanisms to do so—as automatons, brainwashed by an evil fanatic. Amis instead uses his literary virtuosity to paint them as humans—complex, flawed, and real. In doing so, he also implicates corporate Germany of the Nazi era, German voters, anyone who smelled that smell—and who, nearby, did not.

"I do think there are responsibilities involved in taking this subject on. And as with all writing, you have to earn it. But I felt I'd done the emotional suffering spread out over twenty years and I felt that I'd sort of earned the right to address it, just by preoccupation and reading. And you proceed," says Amis, who "gratefully" accepted the duty of writing this novel.

"For a subject like this, you bring everything you've got."

POSTSCRIPT: *Martin Amis died on May 19th, 2023, the same day the film adaptation of this novel had its world premiere at Cannes. The Zone of Interest won two Academy Awards in 2024.*

The whispered words that will blow through the brass in Victoria are cries of anguish from long ago. Words borrowed from harrowing goodbye letters that will fill Alix Goolden Hall with a melodic kind of grief.

Lament of the Wind is the new work by Victoria Symphony composer-in-residence Jared Miller. It will receive its world premiere at the symphony's New Music Festival: Soundscapes and Landscapes, commemorating Canada's 150th. It is a spatial music concert with five works on the program, soundscapes that evoke different landscapes.

The inspiration for *Lament* goes back about a decade, to a blustery day in Jerusalem. Miller was visiting the Holocaust museum Yad Vashem. Toward the end of a visit is the Hall of Names—a memorial to millions of victims in the absence of headstones and cemeteries. There are photos, brief biographies, pages of testimony submitted by survivors, sometimes simply a name taken from deportation or concentration-camp records. For Miller, the unfathomable figure of six million dead came alive with the individual faces and stories. After the emotionally wrenching experience, he stood on a balcony that overlooks the city of Jerusalem. It was very windy.

"I was struck by how much this reminded me of whispers and of sighs and cries of humans," Miller says from Victoria. "In the wind I could hear the rustling and whispers of these people who perished."

Miller, now twenty-eight, was born in Los Angeles and grew up in Burnaby, B.C. He divides his time between New York, where he is finishing his doctorate at Juilliard, and Victoria, where he is in his third and final year of his composer-in-residence appointment. His maternal grandparents, who were Jewish, escaped Poland shortly before the Second World War, fleeing to Kazakhstan.

"My mom told me that Muslims saved my grandparents' life basically at one point. They took care of them, which I thought was a really poignant and beautiful thing to learn about my family," Miller says.

A great-uncle survived Auschwitz and immigrated to New York. A great-aunt was smuggled out of the Warsaw Ghetto in a garbage can. "She was very small," he says.

But most of their relatives were not that fortunate.

"By my mom's calculation, I could have a total of seventeen great-aunts and -uncles plus great-grandparents on both sides, but they were all murdered—shot in mass graves, died in Treblinka,

Buchenwald, and Auschwitz. Some perished in the Warsaw Ghetto Uprising."

So, music. Contemplating this commission, Miller's brain—and heart—kept returning to that windy balcony. He began researching, using Yad Vashem's archives. One of the things he found were letters written by a couple imprisoned in a ghetto in Lithuania in 1944; they were farewell letters to their sons, who had escaped in 1940.

Lament of the Wind was written to evoke those heartbreaking letters, that windswept visit to Yad Vashem.

The composition, a full-orchestra piece running about fifteen minutes, calls for the brass players to whisper some of the text of those letters through their instruments; tormented words murmured through trumpets, trombones, a tuba.

Miller, who experimented with different ways of creating the crying sound of the wind, has some musicians blow across the tops of glass bottles to create an effect that sounds like winds blowing. He tuned the glass bottles, filling them with different levels of water to get those different notes. He also uses slide whistles, which produce a sort of crying, sighing effect.

The staging is also key to the piece. All of the musicians begin onstage, but at a certain point in the piece the brass players leave the stage and situate themselves at different places in the hall, so the audience is submerged in the melancholy. And the piano player, who also begins onstage, ends by repeating a lyrical solo on a different piano, out of sight.

"It sounds like a distant memory when it's played again off-stage," Miller explains.

The sorrowful, ominous piece has its world premiere at a tumultuous political time.[1] This is not lost on Miller, a dual citizen.

"I think what's going on in the States right now is absolutely terrible," he says. "It's terrifying to see attitudes that have been around for a long time be given the authority to come out of the woodwork and given support even by the government in their first attempt at the Muslim ban. I think it's frightening.

"At the same time, I think it's really heartening to see so many Americans who are standing up to it and protesting," he continues. "I hope that people can continue to have the energy to do that."

---

[1] This was early on in Donald Trump's first term as U.S. president.

The refrigerator door in David Schaffer's modest Vancouver kitchen is plastered with photographs of his family, mostly his grandchildren. There are nine of them: seven in Toronto, two in Vancouver—all of them miracles.

Stuck with magnets to the side of that fridge are various phone numbers, instructions about how to recognize a stroke or heart attack, and lighthearted, motivational messages. "Don't Kvetsch Be Happy!" is the boldest among them. And a bit below it, in bright red, "If you obey all the rules you miss all the fun."

A couple of hours after I notice these sweet little messages, I hear Schaffer, eighty-eight, use some of those same words. He is explaining to an artist, a film crew, and an academic, in his precise and philosophical Yiddish-accented way, what not obeying the rules has meant for him. It has meant this kitchen, those grandchildren, his life.

"If we had followed the rules," he says, "I would not be here to tell the story."

Schaffer is telling his story of surviving the Holocaust as part of a Canadian-led international project that involves the Anne Frank House in Amsterdam and other institutions in the Netherlands, Canada, Germany, the United States, Britain, and Israel. Three graphic novelists have been teamed up with survivors on three continents to create three books[1] meant to teach this vital history lesson to high school students in a way that will beckon and penetrate, and not simply horrify.

It is the brainchild of Charlotte Schallié, chair of the Department of Germanic and Slavic Studies at the University of Victoria. As part of her work in Holocaust studies, Schallié has interviewed many survivors. These testimonies are essential, she knows. But for educational purposes, she wanted to create something that would do more than serve as archival proof; something that would jump out at students and get through to them, make them want to learn about this part of history and the implications for contemporary human rights. She wanted something they could consume on a more interactive level, too.

"I felt, What are we doing with these testimonies? They're ending up in archives, and how do we continue to make them relevant?" Schallié explains in an interview, making it clear that eyewitness testimonies are vital and valuable. But, she added, "I felt we need to find something else, new approaches to testimony

---

[1] They ultimately became part of a single book.

collections, telling the story of the Holocaust in a richer, deeper way, and more meaningful way."

Schallié has a son, and at some point while pondering this, she took note of his passion for graphic novels. And she thought about *Maus* and the strong impact that Holocaust story has consistently had on her students. Schallié had her idea.

Each of the three artists has the freedom to explore their own vision in the three digital[2] graphic novels. Schallié hopes the books may be published in physical form, too.

The project addresses another issue related to this field of historical study. Most of the visual material we have from the Holocaust is photography produced by perpetrators, Schallié explains. With artists creating illustrations drawn from the memories of the victims, a different image—one from the survivors' perspective—can emerge.

For about four years, Schallié, whose own grandmother was murdered at Auschwitz, worked to find partners for the project. They now include the Canadian Museum for Human Rights (which will help create a teacher study guide and lesson plan built from survivor testimonials and is planning a visual storytelling conference at the museum[3]), the Vancouver Holocaust Education

---

[2] The stories were published together in physical form as the book *But I Live: Three Stories of Child Survivors of the Holocaust.*

[3] The conference did not take place, but in late January 2025, CMHR hosted an online workshop for Holocaust educators that included the educational resource materials created for *But I Live.*

Centre, and other international institutions (such as the afore-mentioned Anne Frank House).

Then, Schallié had to find funding, and finally, survivors and artists.

This was a race against time and memory. Many of the still-living survivors are suffering from some type of memory loss. But with help from her partners, Schallié was able to find storytellers for her urgent project on three continents.

In Amsterdam, German-born brothers Nico and Rolf Kamp, who were hidden in thirteen places during the Second World War, are working with Israeli comics artist Gilad Seliktar, whose maternal grandmother lost her entire family—they were murdered at the Treblinka death camp—while she managed to flee Poland to safety. There is a Canadian connection here—the couple who hid the Kamps for the longest period of time, Regina and Hendrikus Traa, immigrated to Winnipeg in 1954.

In Israel, survivor Emmie Arbel, who was born in The Hague, is working with Munich-based graphic novelist Barbara Yelin. Yelin, who is not Jewish, wrote her 2014 graphic novel *Irmina* after learning that her late grandmother had been a Nazi sympathizer.

And Schaffer is working with Miriam Libicki, who is based in the Vancouver area and whose paternal grandparents survived the Holocaust.

Libicki, thirty-eight, was born in Columbus, Ohio, and moved to Vancouver in 2002, where she attended Emily Carr University and the University of British Columbia. Her publications include a book of graphic essays, *Toward a Hot Jew*; the autobiographical *Jobnik!: An American Girl's Adventures in the Israeli Army*; and *Ruchie's Job*, about two female prisoners at Auschwitz, which is dedicated, in part, to her grandparents, "whose dry survivor humour I am eternally indebted to," she writes.

Libicki was the 2017 writer-in-residence at the Vancouver Public Library.

"I'd really like to do justice to David's great storytelling ability and the very visual and sensory details," she says.

David (Dago) Schaffer's story begins in 1931, when he was born in the village of Vama, Romania, where his family lived on a large plot of land on which they grew fruits and vegetables and operated a general store. David was a good student who loved school. But in 1939, a few weeks into grade two, he was visited at home by his teacher, who sorrowfully and reluctantly told his parents that, as a Jew, David could no longer attend school.

Thus began an unimaginable years-long trauma for the Schaffers—displacement, starvation, beatings, hard labour, humiliation. They hid in forests and slept in barns. They froze, they roasted, they were dehydrated and maimed. There was death all around them. "I cannot count the number of times I was truly afraid for my life," Schaffer recounts in his memoir, *One Shall Not Be Tested*, which was written as part of a Holocaust memoir project at Vancouver's Langara College.

Libicki read the memoir before meeting Schaffer. That reading inspired some early images she will likely work with, such as a story he tells about his footwear.

His family exiled and starving, David goes into the wheat fields after the harvest to collect spikes that had been left behind. He is about eleven, a growing boy, and has no shoes that fit to protect him from the bits of straw that poke out of the ground and feel like nails on his feet. For protection, he fashions shoes out of rags. But the rags keep falling off, and there is no string or rope. So he uses the only thing he can find to tie his rag shoes to his feet—barbed wire.

There are, perhaps improbably, some big laughs during their interviews. Schaffer jokes a lot; he is a cheerful and optimistic soul, even when telling horrific stories from his wartime childhood, such as being terrified as a Romanian soldier on horseback used his long sword to search his little bag, inside which were hidden a few tobacco leaves—contraband. "You cannot imagine how scared I was, and I cannot describe it to anybody," Schaffer tells Libicki.

Over two days, she listens, takes notes, and sketches in her notebook. Schaffer shows her old photos and documents. A documentary crew films the proceedings for another aspect of the multipronged project,[4] and Schallié takes notes and photos with her phone.

The interviews take place in early January. All agree that recent antisemitic sentiment and attacks, including a multiple stabbing

---

[4] Chorong Kim's short documentary "If We Had Followed the Rules, I Wouldn't Be Here" was completed in 2020.

at a New York rabbi's home during Hanukkah,[5] have brought new resonance to the project.

"Even though I have survivors in my own family I was like, 'Oh well, that's been done. *Maus* is the biggest graphic novel in the world. I should go do other things because I don't want to be just another person who's just doing just another Holocaust story when a Holocaust story is one of the most famous graphic novels in the English language,'" Libicki says. "I think that I changed my mind about that because I do feel it's more urgent now."

For Schaffer, the recent headlines have been particularly hard to take.

"I get frustrated when I hear those news and people try to pretend that it didn't happen or to explain . . . the guy's crazy, the guy's extreme," he says. "But you know, it's like a flame. A little burst-up, and when it becomes a big flame, you can't quench it anymore."

And as difficult as it is to recount these memories—the interviews leave him bone-tired—Schaffer knows how crucial it is.

"This is why I told the story," he says. "I don't like to tell the story, and it kind of stirs me up. But it needs to be done."

---

[5] In December 2019, five people were stabbed during a knife attack at a Hanukkah party in a rabbi's home in Monsey, New York. One of the victims later died.

POSTSCRIPT: *The project became a book,* But I Live, *published by the University of Toronto Press imprint New Jewish Press in 2022, after a member of the team read this story. "If not for your article in* The Globe and Mail *about what Charlotte was doing with the graphic testimonies,* But I Live *would not have come to be," an acquisitions editor there told me. The book has won several awards, including the Canadian Jewish Literary Award for Biography in 2022.*

Ask director Daniel Schubert about the impetus for his film, and he flashes back to the violent 2017 rally in Charlottesville, Virginia, with its neo-Nazis and white supremacists. Three and a half years later, antisemitic attire spotted on rioters in the attack on the U.S. Capitol offered yet more proof to Schubert that his film was needed more than ever.

"I felt like it was my duty, basically," he says.

Schubert's short film is a deeply personal one, documenting a family story.

His grandmother, Martha Katz, is a survivor of the Auschwitz concentration camp, where more than 1.1 million people were killed. Schubert, who was born in Winnipeg and lives in Vancouver, has wanted to record her story for years. After hearing the chants of "Jews will not replace us" in Charlottesville, he got to work. He was also alarmed by surveys showing an ignorance of the Holocaust, especially among young people.

"My purpose in telling her story was to raise awareness but also show the resilience of my grandmother, who at ninety-one is still as tough as ever after going through what can only be described as unimaginable," says the thirty-six-year-old Schubert.

So he travelled to Los Angeles, where his grandmother lives, to ask her some hard questions and revisit her excruciating history. She and four siblings survived the Holocaust, but her parents and two little brothers did not. Her father, she later learned, died right after he was liberated.

"I don't know how I'm alive," Katz says in *Martha*, Schubert's twenty-one-minute film, produced by the National Film Board of Canada.

In the film, we see Katz teaching her daughter, Schubert's mother, how to make cabbage rolls as her own mother used to do in the old country, Czechoslovakia. They were deported to the concentration camp when Martha was fourteen. "We would never go back home," she says in the film.

The notorious Nazi Josef Mengele, known as the "Angel of Death," played a key role in her survival—a shocking story she recounts for her grandson.

Then Katz and Schubert visit a Holocaust museum, where she hears a distressing piece of information about how long, in some instances, the gas chamber process took from beginning to end.

"That was too long," she says. "Too long for my mother."

Martha Katz was taken to the camp from her home in what was then Czechoslovakia when she was fourteen.

In that moment, Schubert quickly reverted from filmmaker to grandson.

"I felt very sad for her—and I felt guilty that I put her in that position," he says.

In an interview shortly after the January 6th riot,[1] Schubert mentioned the "Camp Auschwitz" sweatshirt one of the Donald Trump supporters was wearing and other offensive Holocaust-related T-shirts spotted in the unruly crowd.

"It's so horrible that it's comical," Schubert says. "Why would someone do that? It's something I'll never understand."

He says he's concerned about a new wave of antisemitism spreading in online echo chambers such as YouTube and Twitter.

"I think that new art is needed more than ever now, because if those [surveys] are true—that young people don't know what [the Holocaust] is—of course we need new art, and we need new voices to come out."

Schubert says he hopes his film finds its way into the school system—and along with it, his grandmother and her story. "Maybe her sense of humour will make a difference on a kid," he says. "Maybe it's more relatable than textbooks."

---

[1] During the January 6th, 2021 attack at the U.S. Capitol, one of the people involved was wearing a "Camp Auschwitz" hoodie. He was eventually sentenced to seventy-five days in prison. He was pardoned by Donald Trump in January 2025.

I can think of a few things that could benefit anyone involved in orchestrating the shameful stunt of sending planeloads of desperate, unsuspecting migrants from Florida to Martha's Vineyard in Massachusetts. For instance: sitting them down for six hours and thirty-eight minutes to watch Ken Burns's *The U.S. and the Holocaust*, which aired on PBS.

I'm unsure anyone who hatched this cruel plan has ever watched a minute of PBS, seen a Ken Burns documentary—or seen a documentary, period—but this three-part series should be required viewing for them. (For anyone, really.)

The central point of the documentary (co-made with Lynn Novick and Sarah Botstein) is that while Americans might see their country as a haven for immigrants, and a saviour during the Second World War, the U.S. in fact closed its doors pretty tightly during that critical period—to Jews, in particular. The State Department, lobby groups such as one called America First (sound familiar?), and average Americans didn't want Jews entering the country. When asked two weeks after Kristallnacht in 1938 whether the U.S. should allow more Jews into the country, 70 per cent of respondents said no.

"The exclusion of people and shutting them out has been as American as apple pie," says historian Peter Hayes, in episode one.

(Canada is not the focus of this project, but we do earn a mention in our turning away of MS *St. Louis*, filled with hundreds of Jewish refugees, who were then sent back to Europe.)

Episode two opens with a scene from a Nazi rally, before the war but after Hitler had made his thoughts about the Jews clear.

"You will make a statement as to whether you consider my work to be right, whether you believe that I have been diligent, that I have spent my time decently, in the service of my people, and thus entitle me to say that what I am declaring here and now is what Germany desires, what the German people desire."

A roar of approval fills the packed house, as the crowds stand, arms outstretched.

It was particularly chilling to watch that scene shortly after photos emerged of an Ohio Trump rally where some attendees stood in a similar pose. Even if their outstretched arms in 2022 included a pointed finger, associated with Donald Trump's "America First" rallying cry, it was a stomach-turning image.

The Burns documentary is about history, but it is also a warning about what is happening now. Not just the references to Charlottesville's Unite the Right rally ("Jews will not replace us!")

and the January 6th insurrection, including the guy in the "Camp Auschwitz" sweatshirt, but about increasingly alarming attitudes toward immigrants.

The parallels are striking. Sickening.

During the Second World War, Americans were concerned about the influx of Jews, that they were being "replaced"—the narrator emphasizes this word, surely a nod to the Great Replacement Theory that certain far-right, white nationalist elements have adopted.

In 1941, U.S. senator Robert Reynolds stated, "If I had my way, I would today build a wall about the United States so high and so secure that not a single alien or foreign refugee from any country upon the face of this Earth could possibly scale or ascend it."

It was a humanitarian crisis, yet there was great reluctance to help. There were open calls for the status quo—a "white, gentile-ruled United States." There was suspicion about German-Jewish refugees entering the U.S.

"Something curious is happening to us in this country and I think it is time we stopped and took stock of ourselves," wrote first lady Eleanor Roosevelt. "Are we going to be swept away from our traditional attitude toward civil liberty by hysteria?"

Something is happening—again, still—in the U.S. There is probably a better word for it than "curious."

It should be shocking to every American, to every human being, that officials paid by tax dollars—that anyone, in fact—devised this nasty scheme for these migrants.[1] That others agreed to it, carried it out. That human beings approached these vulnerable people, lied to them, loaded them onto planes, and dumped them not where they were told they were going.

And these prankster perpetrators maybe even laughed, among friends, about it. And in the case of Mr. Trump, claimed that Florida governor Ron DeSantis had stolen the idea from him. Mr. Trump wanted the credit.

This is the country that put children in cages, children who want to live in America. *Well, who sends a child out alone to try to cross a border?* some people tut-tut.

I'll tell you who: desperate parents willing to do the unthinkable for a shot at safety for their children, a good life. It happened during what we now call the Holocaust. And it's happening now.

Historian Deborah Lipstadt says in the film, "The time to stop a genocide is before it happens."

The time to stop anti-immigrant madness is before it happens. The next best time is now.

---

[1] In September 2022, Florida governor Ron DeSantis flew about fifty asylum seekers from Texas to Martha's Vineyard. This relocating of migrants to a Democratic stronghold area was seen as a political protest against President Joe Biden and Democrats' immigration policies, a stunt to dump the problem—and the migrants themselves—onto Democratic doorsteps. DeSantis noted that Florida was not a sanctuary state and it was better for the migrants to be sent to a sanctuary jurisdiction. "Every community in America should be sharing in the burdens," he said.

The most distressing thing about Kanye West's recent antisemitic outburst was not what the rapper said. It was the response.

The justification, rationalization, excuses. The defence. The eruption of finger-pointing. The antisemitism-splaining from people who do not know what it feels like to be its target.

The hip-hop artist now known as Ye posted on Instagram that rapper and record executive Sean "Diddy" Combs was controlled by Jews. And then on Twitter, Ye wrote that he was going to go "death con 3 On JEWISH PEOPLE." His Twitter and Instagram accounts were locked, but not before that tweet received more than forty-two thousand likes.

What happened next is the interesting part.

Some tried to explain the antisemitism by pointing to Ye's bipolar disorder. Mental illness presents differently in different people, but it does not make racism acceptable. Most people who suffer from mental illness do not post antisemitic garbage on Twitter.

But antisemitism has been normalized. How else can you explain that after all this—and the revelation of Ye's further antisemitic ramblings in an interview with Fox News host Tucker Carlson, which had been carefully edited out—an official Republican Twitter account did not delete this (already icky) tweet: "Kanye. Elon. Trump."[1]

Conservative author and pundit Candace Owens—who recently joined Ye in wearing shirts emblazoned with "White Lives Matter," which the Anti-Defamation League calls a white-supremacist hate slogan—said, "If you are an honest person, you did not think this tweet was antisemitic." Also, this: "It's like you cannot even say the word 'Jewish' without people getting upset."

Ye's tweet gave voice once again to an ancient and dangerous antisemitic trope used by, yes, the Nazis: conspiracy theories about shadowy secret cabals of Jews controlling the world (or at least the media). Today, a coded way of expressing antisemitism is to call Jews "globalists" (as in Jews are loyal to each other as a group across the globe and not to their individual countries).

In the fallout, it was claimed that when people tweet other racist things, the world doesn't erupt—but if someone says something against the Jews, watch out. Specific to Ye, people noted that the rapper had been saying all kinds of horrible stuff for a long time (true), but it was only when he targeted the Jews that he was silenced.

---

[1] I guess the Republican Twitter account was more prescient than I was.

The Atlantic's Yair Rosenberg wrote about what he called a catch-22 for Jews. If they say nothing when confronted with such prejudice, the hatred spreads. But if they say something, and there are consequences for the antisemite, he/she uses that as evidence to back up their antisemitic worldview.

There was once a point—in particular, when the horrors of the Holocaust became well-known—when it felt like anti-semitism had become, at the very least, socially unacceptable. We are no longer there.

"It's tough these days not to sense an encroaching darkness," writes Dara Horn in her book *People Love Dead Jews: Reports from a Haunted Present.*

"I had mistaken the enormous public interest in past Jewish suffering for a sign of respect for living Jews," the U.S. author wrote in the introduction. "I was very wrong."

One of the smartest people on the topic of contemporary antisemitism is the British writer David Baddiel, author of *Jews Don't Count*, which explores how antisemitism has fallen through the cracks of modern identity politics and anti-racism campaigns, and how Jewish people often lack the allies that other marginalized groups can rely on. "Kanye West's threat to Jews," he argued on Twitter, "is as ever based on a myth of Jewish power, a myth believed across the political spectrum . . . [that] Jews are powerful so attacking them is punching up and concern for them in the face of it unnecessary." There was a feeling, voiced by the comedian Sarah Silverman in response to Ye's tweet, that allies were silent. Her observation further fuelled the social media war. Groups who are and should be allies when it comes to fighting racism and social injustice wound up at each other's virtual throats. It was ugly and at cross-purposes.

I can picture the real racists and antisemites watching this all go down, having a laugh—all the way to the ballot box, perhaps.

I happened to be in Winnipeg when much of this took place. It was hard not to think about it as I wandered the halls of the Canadian Museum for Human Rights, the section on the Holocaust in particular.

"Antisemitism is a destructive set of beliefs that regards Jews as both inferior and threatening to non-Jews. It existed long before the Holocaust and persists to this day," one of the wall plaques stated.

I was particularly struck by this quote from Holocaust survivor and Nobel Peace Prize winner Elie Wiesel: "There may be times when we are powerless to prevent injustice, but there must never be a time when we fail to protest."

POSTSCRIPT: *In February 2025, West made headlines again as he posted new antisemitic and other severely offensive comments online, including declaring that he's a Nazi who loved Hitler. He ran an ad during the 2025 Super Bowl that took viewers to his website selling swastika t-shirts. More antisemitic posts followed.*

NOVEMBER 2022

A well-meaning Vancouver city councillor, wanting to show solidarity with a Jewish community dealing with a rise of anti-semitism, introduced a motion to officially adopt the working definition of antisemitism proposed by the International Holocaust Remembrance Alliance (IHRA), which calls anti-semitism "a certain perception of Jews, which may be expressed as hatred toward Jews. Rhetorical and physical manifestations of antisemitism are directed toward Jewish or non-Jewish individuals and/or their property, toward Jewish community institutions and religious facilities."

The main issue is the illustrations of antisemitism that follow, more than half of which deal with Israel. One example: "Denying the Jewish people their right to self-determination, e.g., by claim-ing that the existence of a State of Israel is a racist endeavour."[1]

---

[1] Other examples meant to illustrate the IHRA definition of antisemitism

The definition explicitly states that Israel should be held to the same standards as other nations. Holding Israel to account is fine. Holding Israel to account in a way that is out of proportion to other countries is antisemitic. Holding Jews collectively responsible for actions of the State of Israel is also defined as antisemitism.

Several organizations expressed their opposition in writing, including the Union of British Columbia Indian Chiefs, the BC Civil Liberties Association, and Independent Jewish Voices Canada.

Among other concerns, there were worries of a chill to free speech if the motion passed. Speakers said they feared being labelled antisemites for sharing their political opinions. Some in favour, however, noted that the IHRA definition has previously

---

include: making stereotypical allegations about Jews or the power of Jews as a collective—such as the myth about a world Jewish conspiracy or of Jews controlling the media, economy, government, or other societal institutions; accusing Jews as a people of being responsible for real or imagined wrongdoing committed by a single Jewish person or group; denying the fact, scope, or mechanisms of the Holocaust; accusing the Jews as a people or Israel as a state of inventing or exaggerating the Holocaust; applying standards to the State of Israel that are not expected of other democratic nations; holding Jews collectively responsible for the actions of the State of Israel. As you can see, the examples used to illustrate the definition would come into play in a very large way about a year after this column was published.

been adopted by countries around the world, including Canada. And it is the Jewish community that gets to define its oppression, some said.

In council chambers, Palestinian Canadians spoke of being dispossessed from their homeland and unable to return. They worried that the IHRA definition would prevent them from speaking about their heartbreak—or voicing legitimate concern about Israel. "This tells the Palestinians that our voices are not valued," said Hanna Kawas, chairperson of the Canada Palestine Association.

Jewish Vancouverites also told heartbreaking stories. One rabbi spoke about having to install bulletproof glass at his synagogue after its previous location was firebombed. A woman woke up to find a swastika drawn in the snow outside her home. Council heard about swastikas etched into wet cement and anti-Israel graffiti spray-painted on the sidewalk outside a synagogue—the kind of conflation this definition calls out.

One speaker, in voicing his opposition to the definition, ironically gave a compelling argument for adopting it: when there is trouble in Israel, he said, global antisemitism increases. That is exactly the problem this definition seeks to address: to suggest Jews in general are responsible for what happens in Israel is itself racist.

At this point you may be asking yourself: why is Vancouver city council spending all this time and energy—physical, emotional— on this geopolitical issue? In particular when the city is facing numerous crises: housing, health care, drug-related deaths.

It's a good question.

I understand the thinking behind the motion. There is a concern that with antisemitism being taboo (although scarily less and less so these days), some people might use anti-Israel statements to express what is really antisemitism and attack Jews in general.

And I understand what Jews are feeling; I, a Canadian Jew, feel it, too. Unnerved by what is happening. Kanye, Kyrie Irving, Dave Chappelle. It's feeling pretty lonely out here for Jewish people. There's a real sense that nobody has our backs.

But did Vancouver really need to adopt this definition? Listening to the debate, I was struck by divisions growing ever deeper, even within this little Canadian Jewish community. There are not that many of us.

I worry, as some of the speakers did, that going this route might only lead to an increase in antisemitism. Which itself speaks to the problem. Why should I be worried that discussing antisemitism should lead to more of it?

And what about all the other groups dealing with discrimination: Indigenous, Asian, Black, Muslim, LGBTQ Vancouverites?

One rabbi in favour of the motion said he felt traumatized by the debate. I felt traumatized, too. All of these people just wanting to live in peace without fear of brutality and loss because of who they are—Palestinian, Jewish, Canadian.

I also felt gaslit by some of what I heard, including the person (who did not identify himself as Jewish or Palestinian) who declared that there is very little antisemitism in Canada. I wish that were true.

In the end, the motion was adopted, with one councillor voting against it, one absent, and two abstaining.

I don't think it matters. It feels like more damage has been done.

Imagine being afraid to see a doctor. Not because of a deep-seated irrational fear or bad previous experience or because you are worried about a diagnosis . . . but because of what you've heard some doctors at the local medical school say about people like you.

In 2021, Ayelet Kuper, an Israeli-born Canadian physician and scientist, was appointed senior adviser on antisemitism by the Temerty Faculty of Medicine (TFOM) at the University of Toronto. The position was created in response to reports of increasing antisemitism affecting Jewish students, staff, and faculty.

In 2022, Dr. Kuper published a report in the *Canadian Medical Education Journal*. And it is shattering.

In "Reflections on addressing antisemitism in a Canadian faculty of medicine," Dr. Kuper wrote that she had personally experienced "many" instances of antisemitism, including being told that all Jews are liars; that Jews lie to control the university, the faculty, or the world; that they lie to oppress or hurt others, and/or for other forms of gain; and that antisemitism can't exist because everything Jews say are lies, including any claims to have experienced discrimination She told *The Globe and Mail* that it is the most difficult paper she has ever written.

The report recounts incidents she was told about, witnessed, or encountered herself. The culprits included faculty, and as she calls them, learners.

In what Dr. Kuper calls classic discriminatory victim blaming, she writes that antisemitism at TFOM has been "carefully reframed" as political activism against Israel, relating to its treatment of Palestinians. She was repeatedly told that the current environment of growing antisemitism at the faculty was triggered by the spring 2021 war in Gaza.[1] That does not jibe with the rise in antisemitism at TFOM, which goes back at least three years, she writes.

She notes that in the years before the war in Gaza, she overheard faculty colleagues complaining about "those Jews who think their Holocaust means they know something about oppression."

---

[1] In May 2021, a major outbreak of violence took place between Israel and Palestinians that included rocket attacks on Israel and Israeli air strikes in Gaza. Over 11 days, about 260 Palestinians were killed, about half of them civilians, including 66 children. Thirteen people were killed in Israel, including two children. A ceasefire between Israel and Hamas went into effect on May 21st, 2021.

Dr. Kuper, a descendant of Holocaust survivors, writes that she was "berated" for speaking about intergenerational trauma and told that Jews were appropriating the term from Indigenous people. (These complaints came from non-Indigenous colleagues.)

Other Jewish faculty and learners have been silenced when trying to speak about their personal or family histories of discrimination. White Jewish students, she writes, were told by peers that their skin colour means they aren't allowed to claim to have any experience of oppression.

The myth of Jewish power is very much at play: Dr. Kuper has witnessed people at TFOM say or post that Jews control faculty hiring and promotions, as well as Canada's residency matching service.

When a lecture on religious discrimination was instituted at the medical school in 2021, Dr. Kuper was asked by non-Jewish students why the Jewish content was "being forced on the students by the Jew who bought the faculty." They were referring to James Temerty, the philanthropist who, with his wife, Louise, made a large donation to the faculty, which was subsequently named for them. The Temerty family is not Jewish.

Dr. Kuper writes that she was frequently at a loss as to how to escape from what she calls circular reasoning that dismissed her experience of discrimination while dehumanizing her, calling her out as racist for defending herself against racism, and ascribing to her sinister, hidden power.

This is devastating stuff. And it's happening at a medical school that in the period following the Second World War had a quota system restricting the number of Jewish students.

If the current and future doctors of Canada think this way, what do less-educated members of our society think of "the Jews" (a trending topic on Twitter this month)?

This is not just a problem at TFOM. Dr. Kuper says there were instances where Jewish students in other University of Toronto departments were forced to express their beliefs about Israel before being allowed to participate in school activities.

And this is not just happening at the University of Toronto. Dr. Kuper points out that antisemitism has been reported at other higher education institutions in Canada.

Since the article was published, Dr. Kuper says she has heard not only from "many dozens" of Jewish people at TFOM who said her paper resonated with their experiences, but also from Jewish academics elsewhere at U of T and other Canadian universities and medical schools. They have thanked her, she says, for encapsulating their experiences. She has also heard from Jewish Torontonians in other fields who have experienced antisemitism at work.

This as hate crimes against Canadian Jews have risen, and as antisemitism has been spouted by some big-name, influential celebrities in the United States.

Jews aren't always thought of as a marginalized group, but the discrimination is real. And discrimination opens the door to marginalization—and worse.

In her report, Dr. Kuper points out that a large proportion of Jewish Torontonians are Holocaust survivors or their descendants.

In Ottawa, the National Holocaust Monument "recognizes the immense contributions these survivors have made to Canada and serves as a reminder that we must be vigilant in standing guard against antisemitism, hatred and intolerance."

I read that plaque at the monument last weekend, a few hours after reading Dr. Kuper's paper. I pictured some poor old Holocaust survivor in her nineties—perhaps someone who had been the victim of medical experiments at a concentration camp—going to the doctor in good, safe Canada and possibly being subjected to this antisemitism, either blatantly, as a micro-aggression, or worse, as silent dismissal.

For shame.

If you are a Jewish Canadian who is concerned about social justice, believes in the State of Israel, and understands that its existence before the Second World War could have dramatically changed the history of our people, this is a difficult moment. It's painful to watch the current Israeli government, spurred on by its extremist coalition partners, advance its agenda, which includes harmful policies on the treatment of Palestinians and Prime Minister Benjamin Netanyahu's alarming judicial overhaul. But it is also an excellent moment to speak up. Something some of us have been wary of doing.

For Jewish people in the diaspora, our relationship with Israel can be complicated. Even if we vehemently disagree with some of its actions and policies, we can still care deeply for the place and feel to some degree—even if it's subconscious—a reliance on its existence.

The State was established, following a resolution by the United Nations, only three years after the end of the Second World War, which saw six million of us murdered simply for being Jewish.

Even when it became clear in the 1930s what was going on over there in Hitler's Europe, countries around the world, including Canada, kept their doors shut pretty tightly to Jewish refugees. If an Israel had existed then, its doors would have been open.

You can love a country and hate what it's doing. And yet. Even if we disagree with Israel's policies or trajectory—as I do—it can feel difficult to speak up, even dangerous. Beyond the concern that your own community will vilify you for saying such things out loud, there is fear that valid criticism will be co-opted by antisemites. Or by people who believe that Israel should be wiped off the map.

So the stakes of criticizing Israel publicly are high, particularly if you feel protective about the place.

Which is the reason to speak up.[1] To protect it.

The government has introduced a bill that would effectively limit the independence of Israel's Supreme Court.

This has triggered massive protests. They hit a new level on Sunday, March 26th, after Mr. Netanyahu fired his defence

---

[1] There are obviously other reasons to speak up. I was specifically referring here to people who support and are invested in the continued existence of the State of Israel.

minister, who had proposed a delay, warning of potential implications for state security.

When the firing became public, Israelis, in the middle of the night, flooded into the streets across the country. In Tel Aviv, they shut down a major highway. A general strike followed. Flights were suspended, hospital procedures delayed, classes cancelled.

The protesters were not just the usual suspects, but everyday moderate citizens who felt compelled to take a stand.

On Monday, to "avoid civil war," Mr. Netanyahu said that he would put off discussion of the bill until next month. But this is a delay, not a retreat.

Mr. Netanyahu's minister of national security is Itamar Ben-Gvir, who leads an extremist political party and is a partner in the coalition government. This is a man whose views are so abhorrent that, in his home, he hung a picture of the Jewish terrorist who killed twenty-nine Palestinians at a 1994 massacre in Hebron. (He finally took it down to aid his political career.) A man—convicted on charges that include racist incitement against Arabs—who, on election night last November, declared that it was time for "us" to be the landlords of the country. The implication being that others would be the tenants, at best.

When I heard that, I wanted to yell, "Hands off my country."

But of course, it is not my country.

Like many North American Jews, I made a seminal trip to Israel in my late teens. I worked on a kibbutz, visited the Holocaust remembrance museum Yad Vashem, shopped in the vast, rambling Arab market in Jerusalem. This was before the first intifada.

Young and naive, I did not know the facts of the displacement of Palestinians from their homes in 1948 during what they call the Nakba, the Catastrophe.

Though Canadian, the members of my group (all Jewish) were made to feel at home; we understood that Israel was a place that would open its doors to us, should Nazi-like trouble ever rise again. Despite the fact that that summer was only forty years after the end of the Second World War, that possibility felt so far away.

So much has changed since then.

The government could cause irreparable damage to this tiny country that is so beloved, and so despised. And if this goes through, what's next?[2]

The idea that Jews everywhere should be made to answer for Israel's actions is in itself racist. But I feel a responsibility to speak up.

---

[2] In July 2023, the Israeli government passed a law to curb the Supreme Court's ability to review government actions. This was repealed by the Supreme Court in January 2024. The Supreme Court–specific protests largely ended after the October 7th attacks.

Something terrible happened in Poland last week, and it involved a Canadian. University of Ottawa professor Jan Grabowski was just starting his talk at the German Historical Institute in Warsaw when a far-right member of Parliament rushed the stage, attacked the sound system, and smashed Prof. Grabowski's microphone to prevent him from speaking.

The title of Prof. Grabowski's lecture was "The (growing) Polish problem with the history of the Holocaust."

This is a very sensitive topic. In 2021, Prof. Grabowski, who was born in Warsaw—his father was a Jewish Holocaust survivor—was prosecuted under a terrifying law that makes it illegal to accuse Poland of Holocaust complicity. His book, *Night Without End: The Fate of Jews in German-Occupied Poland*, co-edited with Polish historian Barbara Engelking, landed them both in court in a lawsuit supported by the Polish League Against Defamation, which has been described as a nationalist organization close to Poland's government. The two academics were convicted of defamation and ordered to apologize to a surviving relative of a wartime mayor whom the book said helped the Nazis locate hiding Jews. The ruling was later overturned.

Prof. Engelking, who is the founder and director of the Polish Centre for Holocaust Research, has been targeted by the Polish government because of a TV interview in which she said Jews were disappointed with Poles during the war.

At the same time, there is unrest against the right-wing Law and Justice ruling party, with an election coming this year. On June 4th, an estimated five hundred thousand anti-government protesters marched in Warsaw.

This should have been a good year for relations between Poland and Canadian Jews. The city of Lodz has declared 2023 the year of Chava Rosenfarb, a Yiddish writer who, having been born there in 1923, survived the Holocaust and immigrated to Canada. In Lodz, activities have been planned to celebrate her work, including an academic conference to be held in her honour this fall, sponsored by the University of Lodz.

Though she lived most of her life here, Ms. Rosenfarb's work is not well-known in Canada. There is a good chance, however, that you have heard of the man she married, the late Henry Morgentaler—the abortion-rights advocate and physician who was also a Holocaust survivor from Lodz. (They later divorced.)

Among the attendees at the conference will be Ms. Rosenfarb's daughter, Goldie Morgentaler, professor emerita of English at the University of Lethbridge. She learned about the attack on

Prof. Grabowski last week while listening to a webinar about what were known as ghetto benches, where Polish universities forced Jewish students to sit—or stand—at the back of the class. This segregation began in the 1930s—years before the German invasion.

"So I'm listening to a lecture about the 1930s, and suddenly the 1930s are now," Prof. Morgentaler told me.

"It makes me very nervous," she said. "My first reaction was 'I'm not going.' And then I thought, 'Well, that's silly; I'm going. I can't not go.' . . . It's all in honour of my mother. So how can I ignore it?"

What does a conference honouring Ms. Rosenfarb look like, in light of these events? How will historians and students of Yiddish literature feel about travelling to a country where a stage can be stormed in the name of Holocaust revisionism?

This question is not entirely theoretical for me. This month, I will be travelling to Poland—to Lodz, in fact, which is my father's hometown—to do some research. I've asked myself: *Should I be nervous about this trip, because of anything I've written in my Holocaust book? Did I suggest Polish culpability at any point? Could I get in trouble because I wondered where my family's belongings, like my grandfather's violin, ended up after they were deported?*

Of course, many Poles helped Jews—at great danger. Non-Jewish neighbours of my mother's family, for instance, were planning to hide her little brother, but he refused to go with them. He was murdered at Treblinka with his parents.

Prof. Grabowski has bravely continued his important work after his prosecution, at his peril.

Ms. Rosenfarb also continued with her work, in spite of it all. Poems she wrote in the ghetto were confiscated at Auschwitz. When she was then sent to a forced labour camp, she wrote what she could remember onto the bunk where she slept and memorized the words. After the war, she wrote the poems down and sent them to a publisher.

Her daughter told me that when Ms. Rosenfarb died in 2011, she felt she was a failure as a writer. Prof. Morgentaler continues to translate her mother's work into English, hoping to correct that. "I want the world to know about her."

There is a lot the world needs to know.

I couldn't believe what I was seeing: A video promoting Florida governor Ron DeSantis, who wants to be the Republican nominee for U.S. president, ended with his face, surrounded and ultimately replaced by a strange circular spinning symbol. This motif, with its jagged rays emanating from the centre, is known as the Black Sun, or the Sonnenrad. It is a symbol important to and displayed by right-wing extremists, white supremacists, neo-Nazis.

While this emblem might not have been an instantly recognizable Nazi symbol for mainstream observers, I knew what it was immediately. I had just seen it in the flesh, in its original home: a German castle called Wewelsburg that was once a gathering place for the SS.

The image is embedded in the floor of a large circular room in the castle tower, a testament to the creepiness of the place and the SS mission. SS Reichsführer Heinrich Himmler had big plans for Wewelsburg: to turn it into an SS haven—maybe even a spiritual centre—using slave labour from a concentration camp set up nearby for this purpose.

Seeing that twisted sun in situ, knowing it had been installed there by a Nazi architect at the behest of Himmler, knowing it had been viewed and perhaps even worshipped by the sadistic lowest of humanity, and that it continues to be co-opted by repugnant forces—well, what can I say? It was exceedingly distressing. Grotesque.

And it was not the only disturbing encounter I experienced that day, in that place.

I had come to Germany on a pilgrimage, of sorts. My two sisters and I were visiting places we had heard about our whole lives, sometimes only vaguely. With the help of a German researcher, we had located and planned visits to landmarks of our parents' wartime history. They included the meadow where our mother was liberated by U.S. soldiers during a death march in 1945; the hospital where our parents met shortly thereafter; the little city where my eldest sister was born, officially a Displaced Person.

And the highlight: the farm where our father had hidden in plain sight for more than two years, pretending to be someone he wasn't, thanks to forged documents he had obtained in Poland that provided him with a fake name and turned him from Jewish prey into a Christian farm worker. Descendants of the same family still live there.

We were way off the tourist track, in small cities and villages that included Bielefeld, Gutersloh, and Kaunitz. Spots even some Germans have never heard of.

In between our visit to Lippstadt—where our mother had been a slave labourer for a German company in 1944 and 1945—and our visit to our father's farm in a place called Holsen, we had a free day.

Our researcher, Andrea Tebart, suggested a visit to nearby Wewelsburg, a village that is home to a large Renaissance castle with a dark history. The residence, built in the seventeenth century in a striking triangular layout, was taken over by Himmler early in the Nazi reign with the intention of creating a training academy for high-ranking SS.

The SS, short for Schutzstaffel, was the most evil of the evil. The elite Nazi military wing, these were the monsters who ran the concentration camps and conducted mass executions. They were responsible for the so-called Final Solution to the Jewish Question.

Himmler, considered by many to be the most powerful Nazi after Hitler, was made Reichsführer of the SS in 1929 and grew the organization from 250 bodyguards to 52,000 members by the time the Nazis came to power in 1933, and tens of thousands more afterward. Himmler, whose titles included Reich Commissar for the Strengthening of German Ethnic Stock, was in charge of implementing the concentration camp system and thus was the chief architect of the Holocaust.

Using forced labour, Himmler began to transform the castle into what I've seen described as a Nazi Temple of Doom—refurbished to reflect SS aesthetics and ideology, including floors inscribed with runes. An SS guard building was erected next to it.

A concentration camp was established on the outskirts of town for this purpose. The inmates were forced to deepen a moat and strip the exterior walls to enhance the castle's medieval character. To accommodate Nazi motorcades, the main entrance was expanded and an old stone bridge was replaced with a wider concrete one. The slaves had to dig four and a half metres into the solid rock the castle sits on to create a crypt at the base of what has become the notorious North Tower.

The architect Hermann Bartels was planning an even more elaborate SS complex, covering the entire village; the locals were to be displaced. The North Tower was to be its physical and ideological centre.

The concentration camp, known as Wewelsburg/Niederhagen, was initially populated primarily with Jehovah's Witnesses. Other groups on the Nazis' hit list were later brought in, including Soviet prisoners of war—who were treated particularly harshly. At least 1,285 of the 3,900 camp prisoners died—nearly one-third—the result of performing punishing physical labour for 10 to 12 hours a day, while subsisting on only 600 to 900 calories daily. To deal with the high death rate, a crematorium was built on the site.

In June 1941, what became an infamous top-secret gathering

of high-level SS officers took place there. (Hitler never visited.) Widely rumoured but never proven, this meeting may have involved cultish mystical ceremonies. It never happened again. Shortly afterward, the Germans invaded the Soviet Union. After Stalingrad, Nazi attentions were required elsewhere. The Wewelsburg reconstruction was not completed.

Today, this story is told on-site at the Wewelsburg 1933–1945 Memorial Museum and its core exhibition, "Ideology and Terror of the SS," in the former guard house.

It was a good thematic fit for my trip: a look inside the evil that had caused our parents' displacements, the murders of their parents and siblings, and all the trauma that resulted— and has trickled down to my generation. For my sisters and me, this difficult visit was deeply personal. For most visitors— including many school groups—it is a lesson and a warning.

But for some, it is a pilgrimage.

There is no photography allowed in two places in Wewelsburg's North Tower. Visitors are not allowed to take pictures in the creepy circular below-ground crypt with the swastika embedded into the ceiling, the one dug out of solid rock by the slaves.

And there are no pictures allowed in the circular room above it, the SS Obergruppenführer Hall (or Hall of the Supreme SS Leaders).

"We don't want someone posing in front of it," our guide Friederike Horgan explained.

"It" is the so-called Black Sun.

The design—which is, in fact, primarily dark green—is embedded into the marble floor of that hall. With its aggressive spikes emanating from the centre, the crooked sundial design—or Sonnenrad—is reminiscent of the swastika.

While its original meaning is ambiguous, the symbol has been adopted by right-wing extremists and used as a coded sign; a "badge of recognition" in these circles, as the book *Myths of Wewelsburg Castle: Facts and Fiction* (edited by Kirsten John-Stucke and Daniela Siepe and published by Brill) puts it. If you see this circular symbol anywhere, consider it a red flag.

Two recent instances where the Sonnenrad has shown up: on the manifesto posted by the perpetrator of the 2022 mass shooting at the Buffalo supermarket in a Black neighbourhood that killed ten people. The symbol was also found on the bulletproof vest of the terrorist who killed fifty-one people in mass shootings at mosques in Christchurch, New Zealand, in 2019.

Nobody knows where Heinrich Himmler was buried after he was captured by the British in May 1945 and killed himself with a cyanide capsule. His grave was unmarked—like Hitler's bunker (although the location of the bunker is known). The Allies did not want to create shrines for followers of these butchers.

But many right-wing extremists know about Wewelsburg and where this Black Sun originates.

"Are you at all concerned that people might come here to pay tribute?" I asked Ms. Horgan early in our tour. A Ph.D. student in history at nearby Paderborn University, Ms. Horgan told us she would answer when we got to the room in question.

The infamous hall with its jagged floor emblem is furnished with colourful beanbag chairs tossed about—comfy resting spots for school groups, and a bright interruption to the dark drama of this place. (On neo-Nazi Internet forums, there were furious reactions to the beanbag solution, according to *Myths of Wewelsburg Castle*.)

As we sat, Ms. Horgan addressed my question. Yes, she said, this place has become an attraction for some right-wing extremists. The museum estimates about 3 per cent of its visitors come for this sort of perverse pilgrimage. Museum staff are careful about who gets in. Visitors are prohibited from "uttering spoken, written or gesticulated extreme right-wing, racist, antisemitic and sexist remarks," the website warns. Nor can you enter if you display any extreme right-wing symbols or markings—tattoos, T-shirts. Staff are trained to recognize such symbols; there is a catalogue listing the forbidden designs.

Sometimes people try to skirt the rules by skipping the museum and going directly to the North Tower, Ms. Horgan explained. They are not allowed to do this. Some get upset when they are barred entry; a couple of weeks earlier, the police had to be called, she told us.

As if we were in a movie, the big wooden door leading directly into the room from outside lurched open. A couple appeared. They were trying to get inside but were blocked by an iron security gate.

They were heavily tattooed, but I could not see any details of their markings from my beanbag. I did see Ms. Horgan's face as she told them they had to leave, now. If they wanted to see the museum, they had to go through the front desk.

"I knew there was something suspicious because our guide was very agitated and suddenly stopped talking, kept looking at them," my sister Rachel Brass recalled after the fact. "It was very tense."

Ms. Horgan, so kind, then turned to us.

"Obviously it's sad in the sense that you still have these people coming here. You know they're walking past the model of the concentration camp and still, you know, they believe."

When I asked Ms. Horgan later, by email, what made her think the couple fell into the nefarious pilgrim category, she said she couldn't say with absolute certainty that they were right-wing extremists, but she had a strong feeling. There were two clues: They headed straight for the North Tower, bypassing the museum. And they were heavily tattooed with what appeared to be rune symbols.

Earlier that day, I had noticed a solitary man perusing the SS history books in the gift shop, dressed head to toe in camo-gear. I later saw two other couples, also heavily tattooed; one of the men had a jacket carefully folded over his forearm. On that steaming hot July day, that heavy jacket never moved.

Of course tattoos are very common, as is camo-wear. But at this place, in this context, my gut was telling me something, even before our encounter in the SS Obergruppenführer Hall. I tried to tell myself that I was being crazy to think these visitors' intentions were more sinister than ours. But our guide confirmed that it was possible.

"Especially in the summertime when the school holidays are on, they would come more often than in the autumn/winter months," Ms. Horgan told us. "It happens, unfortunately. They do come here. We try to control it as best we can."

The couple that had been barred from entering the North Tower reappeared later in the museum. As they tried to breeze by us in the gallery about the concentration camp, I stood in their way.

"You should have a look at this," I said, pointing to a scale model of Wewelsburg/Niederhagen. They turned and looked, or pretended to. "That's where the crematorium was," I pointed. "Where they burned the bodies."

They didn't say a word. I don't even know what language they spoke. After a few minutes, they silently made their way toward the exit.

"Here we are at Wewelsburg talking about Nazi ideology and it's still around. There's a growing spread of extremism from the far right," my sister Doris Schulman said afterward. "And it really hit me when I saw those people: this is real."

I wonder: Were they really there to pay homage? And if so, could they have had any idea, any inkling, that we were descendants of Himmler's victims? That we were—deep breath—Jews?

One of the horrible thoughts that had consumed my sisters and me as we travelled through that castle was how close it was to the farm where our father lived and worked, pretending to be Catholic to save his life. He was just twenty kilometres away.

This spine-tingling proximity further fuelled my rage that people actually go to Wewelsburg as a pilgrimage. Do they see the other stuff there? The photos of the victims, so malnourished and overworked? The model of the crematorium? What do they think when they pass by the heavy mining cart those poor men had to push up and out of the quarry, filled with rocks? Do they know that sometimes those carts came tumbling down, killing the men?

Do they notice the tube of glue in the museum? The glue that starving prisoners would chew on in a desperate attempt to deal with the incessant, gnawing hunger?

Do they manage to ignore it? Or do they see it—and not mind it?

Are they impressed with the SS uniform manufactured by Hugo Boss? With the skull-and-crossbone "honour rings" and swastika-embossed trinkets?

Do they know that Himmler not only oversaw the extermination camps but visited? Do they know that millions died under his watch? And that sometimes he personally watched?

Does that impress them?

I left, despairing. Over a late lunch of ice cream—we deserved it—we ranted about the need for more Holocaust education.

Then, later that month, that Black Sun video came out. There is someone who worked—well, used to work; he was fired, reports said, after secretly creating the video—for the Florida governor's campaign who thought this would attract voters. This image from the SS castle. How's that for a portent of dark times?

What are the chances of this strange encounter happening? Of three daughters of Holocaust survivors visiting this out-of-the-way museum and running into these people?

For my sisters and me, this was part of an often difficult and disturbing memorial tour as we continue to piece together the tragedies that befell our parents and the grandparents we never met.

For others, the castle visit may be no less important. But for them, not difficult or disturbing. Rather, a tribute. A twisted triumph. And, incredibly, one which some in politics believe holds appeal.

Jews across Canada were preparing for the holiest day on the religious calendar as word was spreading about a major snafu in Ottawa.

Ahead of a twenty-four-hour fast to atone for sins committed in the previous year and ask to be inscribed into the Book of Life for the year ahead, the solemn contemplation was overshadowed by a face-palm-worthy debacle.

It concerns the ninety-eight-year-old Ukrainian Canadian who received a hero's reception in the House of Commons from Ukrainian president Volodymyr Zelensky, Canadian prime minister Justin Trudeau, and everyone else who leapt to their feet.

Unbeknownst to them, they were applauding a guy who fought for the Nazis.

Yaroslav Hunka was honoured in the House for having been a member of the First Ukrainian Division during the Second

World War. Turns out, the unit was also called the 14th Waffen Grenadier Division of the SS.

The Waffen-SS, a quick Google search will tell you, was the military branch of the SS. Its members carried out mass executions, the details of which will stain your soul; it also supplied the notoriously sadistic guards for concentration camps.

"There should be no confusion that this unit was responsible for the mass murder of innocent civilians with a level of brutality and malice that is unimaginable," said the Friends of Simon Wiesenthal Center for Holocaust Studies in a statement. The organization said it was appalled by the standing ovation.

Not exactly the war hero as advertised, Mr. Hunka had volunteered for the unit, reported *The Forward*, citing a blog entry he wrote. In other blog posts, the Jewish publication reported, Mr. Hunka described 1941 to 1943 as the happiest years of his life.

As this information was coming to light, the House Speaker, Anthony Rota, issued a statement, saying the decision to bring in Mr. Hunka, who lives in his North Bay, Ontario, riding, was Mr. Rota's alone. The Ukrainian delegation and Canadian parliamentarians had not been informed.[1]

This apology came out as flowery statements about Yom Kippur flowed from official accounts for the Prime Minister's Office, Mr. Trudeau himself, and others who had given this former (one hopes) Nazi a standing ovation.

---

[1] *Amid outcry, Anthony Rota resigned as Speaker of the House of Commons a few days after Mr. Hunka's appearance.*

As the sun was setting and Kol Nidre—the solemn prayer that begins Yom Kippur—was being chanted by cantors from St. John's to Victoria, the trending topics on X (formerly Twitter) included "The Nazi" and "Waffen-SS."

Oy.

This was obviously an error—a mistake committed without malice. But what an embarrassment. And one with international implications.

Everyone who stood and clapped in the House, maybe with tears in their eyes, will forever be shadowed with this fact: you gave a standing ovation to a guy who was in the Nazi SS, even though the applauders obviously did it in good faith, trusting that the elderly man had been vetted and really was a Ukrainian war hero. Mr. Zelensky and Mr. Trudeau are being chastised for applauding an actual Nazi. (They did, but didn't realize it.)

As I prepared our pre-fast dinner—spaghetti and meatballs (just like in the shtetl)—I felt pretty disheartened. Not just that I, too, had tearily applauded this guy, watching at home, trusting in the system that had honoured him. But I felt sick at the way this debacle was already being twisted and spun by bad actors for political gain.

On a more personal level, consider the utter humiliation to this guy's family. I don't give a fig for Mr. Hunka himself. (If you think that makes me cruel and uncaring, I ask you to investigate how members of the Waffen-SS treated ninety-eight-year-old Jewish men. And women.) But family and friends who must have felt such pride at that moment, who maybe didn't know about Mr. Hunka's past—they don't deserve this.

It would have been so easy to avoid this. A little homework could have prevented this utter disgrace.

If there's any lesson to come out of this sad event, perhaps it's that learning a bit of history can protect us—and from things much more significant than personal embarrassment or political vulnerability. In Ontario, Holocaust education has become mandatory for grade six students. I think there are some older folks who could use a history lesson as well.

PART THREE

The Time After

~

Chasms of grief and hatred.

I remember hearing early on in the conflict that the war might last until the end of the year—2023(!); how horrified I was by that thought. Could this really go on that long? How could we—Palestinians, Israelis, Jews, Muslims, the world—stand it? Any hope that the war in Gaza would end quickly, that the hostages would be returned to safety and the Israeli army would withdraw died at some point, I can no longer pinpoint exactly when, along with thousands and thousands of actual human beings.

There were so many more horrors to come as war continued into a new year—and would continue through a whole other full calendar year, as it turned out, and beyond. As the death toll rose to staggering numbers, and the reverberations continued here in Canada, there was more writing to do, unfortunately, beginning with the first piece in the final part of this collection. This section encompasses columns I wrote about the war and its consequences in 2024, through to the first anniversary of the attacks.

Over the holidays and as 2024 began, I was hearing more and more stories of antisemitism experienced by Jewish people across the country. Each case was upsetting, but collectively, they were alarming. I heard about these incidents from friends and acquaintances and readers who reached out to me, sometimes completely off the record, just wanting me to know what was going on. I heard more stories than I could possibly include in a single column. I also encountered streams of examples on social media, including on Jewish Facebook groups. That's where I learned about Deborah Maes's unpleasant experience with her cellphone provider, which you will read about in the first column in this section. I spoke to Ms. Maes in preparation for that piece, and she was obviously upset. I reached out to the company, which had apologized.

About five months later, in June, I was shocked when I saw a video of a woman named Deborah Maes removing anti-Israel signage at the University of Toronto pro-Palestinian encampment, where she was described as wielding a knife. Was this the same Deborah Maes I had spoken to? It was. What happened to her? Had this woman experienced such anguish that she was driven to this kind of behaviour—with a weapon? Or had this been a terrible misunderstanding?

Later it occurred to me: how many people on the "other side," as we've come to know it, had also been pushed by their own grief and feelings of helplessness to post/say/do something they might never have, had it not been for egregious world events?

I reached out to Ms. Maes in November 2024 and she told me her story: She had gone down to the University of Toronto for a protest in support of students who were feeling intimidated by the encampment. While there, she passed by a sign she felt was egregious. She carries a Swiss Army knife with her in her purse, she explained to me, and she used it to tear down the banner, which was attached to a fence. That's when she was accused by those around her as having brandished a knife. She was questioned by Toronto Police, who investigated. The allegation that she had threatened people with a knife was dismissed and the case was closed. She was never charged. "I'm not a violent person," she said. Shortly thereafter, a hate crime investigation was opened when an anonymous death threat was made against Ms. Maes by telephone. "It's been horrible," she told me. "It's been hell, really hell."

There is a hierarchy of hells. How could the level of horrible being experienced by the Canadians I wrote about in these columns—the physician shut out by his colleagues, the teacher by her union, the university student by her roommates, or the newspaper columnist taking it on the chin regularly on social media and in her increasingly hostile inbox—compare to the actual suffering in the Middle East: the people being bombarded in Gaza; the hostages, still, after all these months, surviving who knew what kind of existence in captivity? If they survived at all. Their families, the hell of waiting. We in the diaspora were in distress, imagining or seeing their suffering. And being on the receiving end of or witness to so many hostilities. Just wanting it all to end, now, soon, sometime, please. But how could I even dare speak of my own suffering-by-association in the same breath as the real agony going on in Gaza and Israel? In the same paragraph, even?

The *Globe and Mail*, thank goodness, made counselling services available to those of us who were affected, in one way or another, from covering this war (above and beyond what is covered in our extended insurance plans, with therapists experienced in such matters). It might sound ridiculous that I would require that kind of help: I wasn't on the ground, seeing anything with my own eyes. I wasn't interviewing shellshocked victims of bombings or families of hostages. But from the periphery, I felt completely caught up in the catastrophe.

My intergenerational trauma had been activated in a way I could never have imagined, and the intensity refused to weaken. Global antisemitism was not abating; the opposite, in fact, and I was quietly spinning out. I wanted on some level to shut it out—but I couldn't stop looking, reading, fearing how bad things could get. Not just because of what I do for a living. But because this is how I live. How I must live, for whatever reason.

Right through the holidays and then back to the 24/7 news grind, I was operating at a high level of anxiety and a low level of sleep, tolerance and hope. I wrestled with it all; frequently angry at myself for being affected this deeply, from the safety of so far away.

Just under two weeks after South Africa brought allegations that Israel was committing genocide to the International Court of Justice. Two days after Israel killed a senior Hezbollah commander in Lebanon; U.S. secretary of state Antony Blinken warned that the Gaza war could spread further across the region; and Pope Francis told diplomats in an annual address that "indiscriminately striking" civilians is a war crime that violates international humanitarian law and called for a ceasefire on every front.

The cops delivering the coffee was the image that went 'round the world. But long before members of the Toronto Police Service handed over the Tim Hortons goodies to pro-Palestinian protesters who have been targeting a highway overpass adjacent to a neighbourhood with a significant Jewish population, many Canadian Jews were feeling unsettled, even unsafe.

To be clear, the officers did not purchase the coffee but dropped it off on behalf of protest supporters who were not allowed on the overpass. Still, it felt like a scalding metaphor.

Protest is essential and the freedom to do so is a key tenet of a democracy, as is freedom of speech. But when protests target Jewish neighbourhoods—rather than, say, the Israeli consulate—it hurts. There are Canadian Jews who feel intimidated, scared. And it's not just on the Avenue Road bridge over Highway 401 in Toronto or the area in Windsor described as "Hebrew Heights."

Canadians who happen to be Jewish are feeling unwelcome in many spaces. Spaces that once welcomed us can now feel hostile. Sometimes it's school, sometimes work.

Ted Rosenberg is a family physician who has pioneered a humane house-call approach for geriatric patients. Until this year, he taught that model to medical students at the University of British Columbia. But he resigned on January 1st, after urging the administration for more than a month to address what he calls a toxic environment of antisemitism. "We as Jewish faculty feel these attacks personally and deeply," he wrote in his resignation letter.

The final straw, he says, was seeing a colleague post an image of Christ in the rubble of Gaza on social media. "People are talking about Christ-killing within this faculty," he told me on Monday from Victoria, where he lives, noting that this is an age-old and dangerous antisemitic trope.

For many of us, aggressive posts from colleagues, friends, and acquaintances (dictating, for instance, what they, non-Jews, define as antisemitic or not, or playing down the horrors of October 7th) are a major source of this distress. Walking into a place we might have once considered a second home (an office, a yoga studio), knowing what the person sitting at the next pod or doing downward dog three mats over has been posting about people like you.

Of course we all have a right to express our opinion. But I think it is important that people understand the consequences, perhaps unintended: some of your fellow Canadians, your friends and neighbours, feel unsafe.

Toronto resident Deborah Maes recently reached out to her cellphone provider, Freedom Mobile, to ask about a plan for upcoming international travel, including Israel. The customer service representative interrupted. "I've never heard of that country. Oh, you must mean Palestine," she recounted to me.

"I thought, 'Oh my God, politics has pervaded everything, even my cellphone company,'" Ms. Maes said. (The company later resolved the issue to her satisfaction. Freedom Mobile, in a statement emailed to The Globe, apologized, saying the comments were unacceptable and that the agent no longer works there.)

At Vancouver's Science World over the holidays, a child-friendly show began with a land acknowledgment that ended with the words "from the river to the sea"—a phrase that some Jews perceive as a wish to remove Jewish people from the land of Israel. (Science World told me in a statement, "These comments were not appropriate, and we apologize for any impact they had on our attending guests.")

Sure, people can vote with their wallets, but shouldn't Jewish Canadians have the right to feel safe taking their kids to a science museum? Or call their cellphone provider without risking the shock of a political sneer?

Over the past three months, I have repeatedly heard Jewish Canadians express a version of "Now I know what it felt like for German Jews in the 1930s."

It's not just the in-your-face protests or rhetoric many Jews find demonizing, including Holocaust inversion (portraying Jews or Israelis as modern-day Nazis). It's being told things like "go back to Poland!" (this happened in Montreal); it's shots fired at a Montreal Jewish school; arson at a Jewish-owned grocery store in Toronto.

We begin emails, "I hope you are as well as possible."

And you know what? We are not. Many Canadian Jews are not well.

You can whatabout this all you want. But why Canadian citizens and residents who happen to be Jewish should be targeted for what the Israeli government is doing in Gaza is beyond me.

Well, it's not really. I think we all know what's happening here.

JANUARY 16TH, 2024

The war has passed the 100-day mark and the Gazan death toll is nearly twenty-four thousand, according to Gaza's health ministry. On January 14th, a Hamas spokesperson said many of the Israeli hostages abducted on October 7th "may have been killed." He said their fate was unknown and blamed this on Israel. In that same broadcast, Hamas played a video of three of the hostages, ending with the words "Tomorrow we will inform you of their fate." The next day, Hamas announced that two of them were dead. The third, Noa Argamani, would be rescued by Israeli forces in June.

For years, the PuSh International Performing Arts Festival has been a highlight of Vancouver's arts scene. I once called it a "beacon of avant-garde light in the dead of winter."

I won't be calling it that anymore. The festival has now added to the darkness of this already tragic, oppressive season.

Last week, PuSh decided to cancel its planned performances of the Canadian play *The Runner* at Simon Fraser University's Woodward's Goldcorp Centre for the Arts. The one-person play, written by Christopher Morris, has received rave reviews, including from *The Globe and Mail*'s J. Kelly Nestruck in 2018.

It tells the story of Jacob, an Orthodox Jewish volunteer whose job is to retrieve body parts in the aftermath of accidents or terrorist attacks in Israel, so Jewish bodies can be buried whole, as religious law demands. In the play, Jacob makes the decision to save a Palestinian woman who was shot in the back after it appears she fatally stabbed an Israeli soldier. As Jacob points out, it's possible she did not do it.

"She's a person, a teenager, a girl," he says, as he is chastised for helping her. That his decision is controversial is part of the critique the play levels at Israel, as I see it.

"It's inhumane what we're doing," Jacob says. "It's not Jewish!"

The Runner was programmed long before October 7th, 2023, when Hamas launched its horrific terrorist attacks on Israeli citizens, provoking the terrible, deadly response by Israel that has since killed tens of thousands of Gazans, according to the Hamas-run health ministry. So was a planned March run at Victoria's Belfry Theatre.

I have not seen *The Runner*, but I've read the script. I see it as a heartbreaking and nuanced contemplation of the issue and, in fact, a criticism of Israeli attitudes and actions toward Palestinians.

The context has changed, but that has only made *The Runner* more relevant, one would think.

But also controversial. In Victoria, there was a protest, the theatre was vandalized—and the Belfry caved, cancelling the production.

At the time, PuSh doubled down, vowing to move ahead with *The Runner*. (Full disclosure: before the debate erupted, I had agreed to moderate a post-performance panel; I had to withdraw for reasons that had nothing to do with the controversy.)

I spoke to Michael Boucher, the director of cultural programs and partnerships at SFU Woodward's, after the Belfry pulled out. He called the decision "artistic intimidation" and said that he did not want to capitulate to it. "I think the arts have lost their backbone if they're questioning this," he said at the time.

Mr. Boucher declined to comment after PuSh's cancellation, but the festival made clear that its statement was "fully independent" from the curatorial viewpoint of SFU Woodward's.

PuSh's reversal came about because the Palestinian-British artist Basel Zaraa said he would pull his art installation *Dear Laila* from the festival if *The Runner* remained.

So curators capitulated not to angry audiences, but to an artist.

Among the subsequent outrage expressed on X was a post suggesting that a more apt name might now be the Push Over Festival.

The more than 380 people who signed a petition calling for PuSh to cancel the play include artists, authors, and booksellers. What kind of world are we living in when it's artists who are calling for art to be censored? How is this different from calls to ban books?

One of the issues the petition cites is that the play exacerbates ugly historical tropes representing Arabs and Muslims as terrorists and notes that all the Palestinians in the play, including the woman Jacob helps, are nameless.

I happen to disagree with the first concern, but that's just my opinion. As for the second concern: if this is the criteria we are going to use for banning works of theatre, programmers are going to have to get busy cancelling all sorts of plays that offer less-than-fleshed-out portrayals of characters.

Also, if we're doing this now, I wonder how Canadian theatre is going to handle *The Merchant of Venice*. You can twist yourself into all sorts of artistic knots about Shakespeare's tragedy, but the fact remains that Shylock, the Jew, is a despicable character. In her book *People Love Dead Jews*, Dara Horn argues that the play is antisemitic, and yet people like herself have "felt obligated . . . to contort this revolting material into something that excused it."

We keep showing it because it is great art. We discuss its problematic portrayal of the Jewish character. We let audiences decide.

Unless the bullies decide for you that you can't see it—and the very people who are supposed to stand up for artistic freedom capitulate to those tactics.

*One day after Benjamin Netanyahu rejected U.S. calls
to scale back the war in Gaza and repeated his
objection to a two-state solution.*

While many of us were shovelling snow or deciding if we could afford to splurge on a head of lettuce,[1] some of our Canadian neighbours were fighting for their families' lives. They have been engaged in a desperate undertaking, jumping through life-or-death hoops as they try to get loved ones out of Gaza—a war zone where thousands have been killed, many more have been injured or displaced, food and water are scarce, medical services are largely unavailable, and conditions are dangerous and deplorable.

Canada has agreed to open its doors to one thousand Gazans who are relatives of Canadian citizens or permanent residents. (Or possibly more; the originally announced cap is not absolute,

---

[1] Food affordability was a major issue in Canada at this time.

Immigration minister Marc Miller said.) The temporary immigration program, which offers three years of sanctuary, stipulates that the Canadian family member—or "anchor"—will be responsible for financial support.

The process has created confusion, concern, and panic. It is a two-stage application. If the first step—an expression of interest—is approved, a second, much more comprehensive step demands detailed information, sometimes from decades ago. Vancouver-based immigration and refugee lawyer Randall Cohn described this to me as absolutely the most onerous standard form he has ever seen.

Applicants are asked to provide employment history from the age of sixteen, with dates, names of their supervisors, any disciplinary problems, and why they quit. This applies to people as old as seventy-nine.

I'm a lot younger than that and I certainly cannot remember the name of my manager at the Don Mills Centre's Body Shop in 1984, or if I ever got in trouble for returning late from my break. And I am not under duress. With all that these people are going through, how are they supposed to remember these details? Why should they have to?

They are also asked to list their scars and injuries. And to disclose all social media accounts—presumably to check for terrorist-supporting posts. Fine. But teenagers sometimes post stuff that is offensive and even awful. And I don't think sharing ill-advised memes should preclude these kids from being given a shot at safety.

Mr. Miller has said that the prospect of a Hamas fighter or commander involved in the October 7th attacks making it to Canada "is probably the most extreme security concern that we have—and I think it's very real," as *The Globe and Mail*'s Marie Woolf has reported.

But of course proper security checks are being conducted on Gazans who want to leave.

As Mr. Cohn explained to me, this level of scrutiny sometimes arises at a later stage in the immigration or refugee process, should the standard screening produce a specific reason for concern. Do we really need to ask every applicant to detail their wounds to ensure Canada is not opening the floodgates to terrorists?

Further, initially announcing the program with a one-thousand-person cap has caused much anxiety. "Families in Canada who are part of this traumatized community . . . are all of a sudden pitted against each other, feeling like they've got to compete to be in that first one thousand," said Mr. Cohn, who is part of several ad hoc groups working on this issue, including the Gaza Family Reunification Program.

Canada has recently welcomed more than 210,000 Ukrainians. While the situations aren't exactly comparable, I think it's fair to ask, Why are there special rules for Gazans?

In 2024, *The Globe* is publishing *A Nation's Paper*, a book of essays examining Canada's history and this newspaper's role as its chronicler. I wrote a chapter about our record on immigration, something of personal interest to me, as my parents were essentially refugees.

I read deeply into the archives about waves of immigrants who came or wanted to come to this place, and the obstacles put in their way by the government or citizens, whose racism was often overt. So many stories depicted hostility toward people wanting to escape a terrible situation elsewhere—people just like us, who wanted to live without fear or starvation.

In many instances, Canada did not get it right. Reading some of these accounts was heartbreaking and maddening. We should not make these mistakes again.

Never forget that Alan Kurdi, the three-year-old Syrian boy whose body was photographed washed up on a beach, died seeking refuge with his family—and that his family had hoped to come to Canada, where his aunt lives.

In a perfect world—and no, the world isn't anything close to it—Canada would make it easier for these people fleeing hellish conditions to find sanctuary here. And eventually, they would be able to return to Gaza, where they can rebuild and live under self-determination. I, like many others (if not Benjamin Netanyahu), hope for a two-state solution with dignity and security for all.

Until then, we should not be making it this difficult for Gazans to find security here, with their families.

Four days after Canada announces it will suspend support to UNRWA, joining the United States. The actions followed information that a few UNRWA staff had participated in the October 7th attacks.

Established by the United Nations after the 1948 war resulting from the establishment of the State of Israel, the United Nations Relief and Works Agency for Palestine Refugees (UNRWA) has cared for some seven hundred thousand Palestinians who fled or were driven from their homes in that upheaval. Operating since 1950, it is the largest provider of aid in Gaza.

Allegations have been made public that at least twelve UNRWA employees participated in the October 7th attacks on Israel. The possibility of such crimes being carried out by employees of a United Nations agency is alarming.

The allegations are contained in an Israeli intelligence dossier obtained by some media outlets. The document lists twelve or thirteen people—reports vary—nine of whom worked at schools as teachers and in other capacities. The others, according to the *New York Times*, include a social worker, a clerk, and a store-room manager.

According to the *Times*, a school counsellor employed by UNRWA is accused of working with his son to abduct a woman from Israel. A social worker is alleged to have distributed ammunition and coordinated vehicles on the day of the attack, and to have helped bring the body of a dead Israeli soldier to Gaza. Three others are accused of participating in the attacks.

The UN has fired nine of the accused. Two are dead.

Some reports and commentators have emphasized the small number of aid workers involved—that this is just twelve or thirteen people out of thirteen thousand UNRWA employees in Gaza. A few bad apples.

That said, the document alleges at least 190 UNRWA workers doubled as Hamas or Islamic Jihad operatives. Further, Israel says that at least 10 per cent of UNRWA's Gazan employees have links to Hamas, which governs Gaza. Hamas is considered a terrorist organization by Canada, the U.S., and several other governments, as well as by the European Union. Membership in the organization is not permitted for UNRWA members.

Even if it was only a dozen people who participated in these attacks, this is egregious. A betrayal. Unforgivable. These allegations demand the utmost scrutiny of the organization, reconsideration of government funding for it, and perhaps its dismantling altogether.

But not now.

Gaza is a war zone teetering on the edge of catastrophe. More than twenty-six thousand people have been killed there so far, according to Gazan officials. The medical system has collapsed. The UN has warned of famine.

UNRWA's duties in Gaza include running schools, health care clinics, and other social services and shelters. It distributes humanitarian aid, which nearly the entire Gazan population now relies on for food, water, and other basic necessities.

Despicable as these allegations are, with so many funding nations initially pulling support for UNRWA in the wake of the allegations—including the U.S. and Canada—the agency has said it will not be able to operate beyond the end of February. Even with Canada announcing plans to allocate funding for Gaza elsewhere, other aid groups have said there is no other organization that can fill a gap left by UNRWA.

Israel has long expressed concern about UNRWA's lack of neutrality and its possible role in indoctrination. On Monday, Prime Minister Benjamin Netanyahu said UNRWA was "perforated with Hamas" and that its schools have "been teaching the doctrines of extermination for Israel—the doctrines of terrorism, glorifying terrorism, lauding terrorism."

And now this. These allegations are sickening.

Pulling funding is a punitive measure. It's understandable. But it's the wrong thing to do in the midst of war and a dire humanitarian crisis.

The employees of UNRWA and their actions demand intense scrutiny. When the dust settles and Israel's offensive in Gaza ends, there will have to be serious discussions about overhauling and possibly replacing UNRWA altogether. But right now, it must be allowed to continue its crucial work. And to do that, it needs money.

Do not punish the starving children of Gaza for the appalling actions of these fraudulent aid workers.

POSTSCRIPT: *In February 2024, UNRWA issued a statement saying that it had not received any evidence from Israel that 10 per cent of its staff in Gaza had links to Hamas or the Palestinian Islamic Jihad. In March 2024, Canada announced it would restore funding for UNRWA. In October 2024, Israel's parliament voted to ban UNRWA from operating within Israel.*

FEBRUARY 15TH, 2024

*Three days after Israeli forces rescued two hostages from Rafah
in an operation that killed more than sixty Palestinians.*

Whether Toronto's Mount Sinai Hospital was a target of pro-Palestinian demonstrators this week, as witnesses felt and politicians have declared, or just a coincidental stop along the way, is a matter of debate as I write this. Perhaps, as some have explained, the protesters who stood outside the hospital as someone scaled the scaffolding with a Palestinian flag, and as shouts of "Intifada!" were yelled through a megaphone and repeated by the crowd, did not know about the hospital's connection to the Jewish community, or stop there for that reason.

Either way, saying that they didn't realize (or care) that Mount Sinai has Jewish ties is not the defensive flex some seem to think it is. Nor is pointing out that this stop was a mere fifteen-minute slice of a four-hour demonstration. Standing outside any hospital and loudly yelling about an uprising is just not okay.

It was at the very least unpleasant, at the worst cruel, to those inside or trying to get there. People who are ill, injured, reeling from treatment, or dying deserve peace and quiet, as do their loved ones who are with them, praying, grieving, hoping. I'll apologize on their behalf if they weren't thinking about Gaza as they live through their own hell. It could also be rattling to health care workers trying to do their life-or-death jobs.

And even if the literal translation of the Arabic word "intifada" is "uprising" or the shaking-off of something, it has a violent connotation for many who recall the events of the Second Intifada, a grassroots terror campaign that sent suicide bombers into Israeli buses, restaurants, and crowded streets, killing more than a thousand people.

To act all surprised and who us? about this feels disingenuous.

One explanation I've seen supporting the protesters' stated unawareness about the hospital's Jewish ties or origins (it was founded when Jewish doctors faced restrictions around practising elsewhere) points out that Mount Sinai is located in Egypt.

Okay. But Mount Sinai is where Moses—possibly, after Jesus, the most famous biblical Jew—received the Ten Commandments.

Even if you don't believe this stuff, or you're not up on your biblical history, this is one of the Old Testament's greatest hits. And the protesters seem to be experts on the history of this region, right? Among the Commandments: thou shalt not kill. What happened on October 7th was horrific. What has happened in Gaza since is horrific. People have every right to protest this bloodbath of a military operation.

But doing it outside a hospital, any hospital, is wrong—and won't help the cause. Olivia Chow is not the mayor of Tel Aviv. Doug Ford has no influence in the matter. And I'm not sure Justin Trudeau has much sway in this geopolitical issue either. But they do have a responsibility to Torontonians, Ontarians, Canadians: to keep us safe.

Some have wagged their finger at those upset by the protest, saying it hardly compares to the devastation in Gaza, including the main hospital in Rafah, which Israeli troops raided on Thursday (searching, they said, for Hamas fighters and hostages' remains). How dare people complain about a bit of discomfort and inconvenience at this one Toronto hospital amid this global catastrophe?

What's happening in Gaza is catastrophic. Absolutely. But Canadians, lucky us, have a right to safety and security here.

And if you're wondering why Jews may have jumped to the conclusion that the protest at Mount Sinai was antisemitic, consider that one of the organizers of the march, Toronto4Palestine, has previously amplified atrocity—and Holocaust denial—on social media. One such post accused the "Je*ish occupation" of lying about what happened on October 7th.

And if they would lie about that, this post went on, is it "likely they may have lied about certain details of a previous big genocide that may have occurred?" Consider also that Memorial Sloan Kettering Cancer Center in New York was loudly targeted in January by pro-Palestinian protesters, upset about a donor.

Many Canadian Jews have felt undone by the events of October 7th.

There are still more than a hundred hostages being held by Hamas. This alone is traumatic, even for those of us who oppose Benjamin Netanyahu and the brutality of his military response. The antisemitism that has arisen since has further traumatized us. Jewish Canadians are feeling vulnerable and scared.

There have been protests outside Jewish restaurants, shots fired at a Jewish school, and the alleged targeting of a Jewish grocery store. Some Canadian Jews have stopped wearing or started hiding Jewish-identifying jewellery.

Please don't "cry me a river" about this. This is unacceptable, full stop. Racism against any other ethnicity would not and should not be tolerated. Why should Jews have to accept it?

So forgive Jews for being on edge here in Canada. But protesting outside a hospital, any hospital, is unforgivable.

Two days after the U.S. vetoes a UN resolution, drafted by Algeria, demanding an immediate ceasefire as the Palestinian death toll surpasses twenty-nine thousand, according to Gazan officials.

Shortly after the October 7th Hamas attacks on Israel, the Frankfurt Book Fair cancelled an award presentation for Palestinian novelist Adania Shibli. It would hold the ceremony at a different time, it said—in a "less politically charged atmosphere."

It was a bad decision, and it was just the beginning. As the atmosphere has become only more politically charged, the cancellations—official or stealth—piled up.

Popular Quebec children's author Elise Gravel had her books moved to closed stacks at Montreal's Jewish Public Library. This followed her posts about the devastation in Gaza, including one that seemed to echo the age-old blood libel aimed at Jews. "The fact that Israel has the largest skin bank in the world, harvested from Palestinians, should be enough evidence for anyone."

Parents can choose not to buy her books or read them to their kids—or to check them out from the library. But they should not be taken out of the library. Or off the shelves. (The library, correctly, reversed its decision after an outcry.)

In the U.S., authors petitioned the literary free-expression organization PEN America over its co-sponsorship of an event featuring Israel supporter Mayim Bialik interviewing an author. Protesters inside disrupted the event, rattling some attendees to the point of tears, PEN said. The irony, right?

The New York–based Jewish Book Council has launched an initiative to track antisemitism in the literary world, including review-bombing, cancellations, and threats of violence.

On social media, people are calling out celebrity artists who signed a letter calling for the release of the October 7th hostages, vowing to stop consuming or reviewing their work.

What's worse, artists are being deplatformed not just for open letters they've signed, or their comments, or their work—but for their allegiances, real or perceived.

The Jewish musician Matisyahu had shows cancelled in Santa Fe, N.M., and Tucson this month, with protests expected and staff refusing to work. "They do this because they are either antisemitic or have confused their empathy for the Palestinian people with hatred for someone like me who holds empathy for both Israelis and Palestinians," he posted.

Here in Canada, Likht Ensemble—two Jewish artists based in Canada who perform music by Jewish composers from the Holocaust and present workshops on the music and antisemitism of Richard Wagner—lost engagements in the aftermath of October 7th.[1] (At least one company hopes to reschedule their work for next season.[2])

Concerns about antisemitism are so pervasive that when two Jewish-Canadian arts festivals did not receive Canada Council grants this year—grants they have regularly received previously, and which were adjudicated in November and December—they wondered if there was a connection.

"I think that they just don't see our community as fitting into any kind of priority group," Chutzpah! Festival artistic managing director Jessica Gutteridge said, noting she was told diversity, equity, and inclusion would be a top priority in the decision-making process. "We're trying to be really broad and diverse, as the Jewish community is, and it's still not getting us anywhere. So what are they looking for?"

Audiences are also encountering these divisions, even at shows meant for laughs. In London, comedian Paul Currie allegedly hounded an attendee, who turned out to be Israeli, out of his show, after the audience member wouldn't applaud the Palestinian flag. "While we robustly support the right of artists to express a wide range of views in their shows, intimidation of audience members, acts of antisemitism, or any other forms

---

[1] I had been scheduled to take part in one of the Likht Ensemble's events cancelled in the wake of the Oct. 7 attacks, an artist talk at Pacific Opera Victoria.

[2] The workshop was not, in fact, rescheduled for the 2025–26 season.

of racism will not be tolerated," the Soho Theatre said afterward.

And two attendees of a recent show at Vancouver's Vogue Theatre told me that comedian Tony Hinchcliffe worked the October 7th attacks into his routine with a joke about beheaded Jewish babies: that as the dying babies' heads were falling to the ground, "The last thing they saw was 'Oh, is that a nickel?' and everyone just laughed," recalls Primo Allon, who was in the crowd. The Vogue did not respond to emails about this, nor did Mr. Hinchcliffe's management.

Artists should be able to express their views, but that ends with hate speech. Free speech is important, but so is safety.

In Australia, hundreds of Jewish writers, artists, musicians, and academics recently found themselves on a list along with personal details leaked by pro-Palestinian activists. I've seen Canadians call for making such lists as well.

We need to hear from artists right now: to help us navigate through this terrible time, to offer hope and remind us of our shared humanity—and, let's face it, for some distraction, too.

It would be a shame if artists are tossed onto the curation cutting-room floor for a stance they've taken, so long as it does not incite hate or violence, or for simply being a member of a specific group.

Israel has announced plans to evacuate Gazans from Rafah, ahead of a planned offensive. U.S. Senate majority leader Chuck Schumer calls on Israel to hold new elections, saying he believes Benjamin Netanyahu has lost his way. Around the world, including in stricken Gaza, Muslims are observing Ramadan.

There's a story often told about Pablo Picasso's *Guernica*. In black and white and shades of grey, his monumental anti-war mural depicts the aftermath of the 1937 German and Italian bombing of the Basque town of Guernica, in support of Spain's nationalists. As the legend goes, when a Nazi officer visited Picasso's apartment in German-occupied Paris, he pointed to the mural.

"Did you do that?" the Nazi asked.

"No," Picasso responded. "You did."

Less well-known is the online literary magazine named after Picasso's masterpiece.

Guernica, a magazine that publishes work about "global art and politics," suffered mass resignations following its publication of "From the Edges of a Broken World," an essay by Joanna Chen, an Israeli writer who translates Arabic and Hebrew poetry and prose.

Born in Britain, Ms. Chen has lived in Israel since she was sixteen. She refused mandatory military service there and volunteers for Road to Recovery, which takes Palestinian children to Israeli hospitals—the same organization, Ms. Chen notes in her essay, for which Canadian peace activist Vivian Silver volunteered, a beloved humanitarian who was murdered on October 7th on the kibbutz where she lived.

In other words, she is hardly a warmonger.

Still, her *Guernica* piece was decried. Not just by some readers but by staffers at the magazine, who volunteer their time—or did, because many consequently quit.

Guernica's now-former co-publisher Madhuri Sastry tweeted that she was "deeply ashamed" of Ms. Chen's "hand-wringing apologia for Zionism and the ongoing genocide in Palestine."

The now-former fiction editor, Ishita Marwah, wrote that by publishing the piece, *Guernica* had become "a pillar of eugenicist white colonialism masquerading as goodness."

Under fire, *Guernica* pulled the essay, saying it regretted having published it and promised a more "fulsome" (improper use of the word, but whatever) explanation soon.

You may be wondering: How awful could this essay have

been? Did it cheer on the killing of thousands of Gazans, including children?

No. "From the Edges of a Broken World"—still archived online—is about navigating this catastrophe as an Israeli who has managed to forge a shaky and, yes, unfairly hierarchical coexistence with Palestinians.

There is one passage in particular that many have pointed to as evidence of the essay's awfulness. Ms. Chen writes about a neighbour who, after October 7th, tries to calm her children, frightened by the sound of warplanes: "I tell them these are good booms."

There are, of course, no good booms in war. These booms are from bombs killing people in Gaza. Ms. Chen knows they are not good. Perhaps the neighbour she quoted does as well. These are the lies mothers tell for their children in wartime. That is what makes this observation powerful: it offers a window into the ugliness of war, even from the safety of the other side.

The piece is critical of Israel and some Israelis. When Ms. Chen recounts a friend admonishing her for giving blood for Palestinians in 2014, she is showing us something disdainful about Israelis.

What was Ms. Chen's great crime? Was it presenting herself as a white liberal saviour? Or was it simply being Israeli and daring to write about her experience?

Online, below a note about the retraction, *Guernica* tells readers about its "uncompromising journalism." It adds: "If you value *Guernica*'s role in this era of obfuscation, please donate."

Can *Guernica* survive this? A more important question: Can free and honest artistic expression survive this moment?

Palestinian artists' voices have been silenced. And it seems impossible to present an Israeli perspective—even a sensitive, nuanced one, like this essay—without being denounced for it.

At the intersection of art and politics now sits a flashing red light that will allow only some voices through. Don't we want to hear all perspectives? To examine and be challenged by the shades of grey amid the often black-and-white discourse?

Picasso's *Guernica* is a protest depicting chaos and grief, including a mother wailing to the skies as she holds a dead baby. To look at it through today's lens is to conjure the hell that Gaza is being subjected to by Benjamin Netanyahu's Israel.

Ms. Chen did not do that.

Nobody's saying her essay is a *Guernica*-level masterpiece. And it presents a perspective from the other side, as it were. But that doesn't mean it should be disappeared.

There is a full-size tapestry replicating *Guernica* at the entrance to the Security Council at the United Nations headquarters in New York. In 2003, a blue curtain was hung over the work, as the U.S. argued for support to invade Iraq. That was a crucial moment when the Security Council, the U.S. government, and everyone watching on TV needed to see that wailing mother and her dead baby.

Art about the Hamas–Israel war is urgently needed. Covering it up is a mistake and a distraction.

POSTSCRIPT: *In April 2024, Guernica's founder Michael Archer posted a statement titled "Moving Forward" explaining that he retracted the piece after some readers were angered by it and "experienced its presence in the magazine as a betrayal."* Guernica's *editor-in-chief Jina Moore, who had published and supported the piece, also left the magazine in the aftermath.*

Good Friday sees scaled-back observances in Jerusalem,
one day after the International Court of Justice orders
Israel to urgently open new land crossings to bring
desperately needed supplies to Gaza.

Nearly six months after the horrific Hamas attacks of October 7th triggered a catastrophic war in Gaza, thousands of Palestinians have been killed; Gazans, including children and pregnant women, are under siege and starving in a human-made famine. Israeli hostages are still being held in Gaza. This week, the *New York Times* published the account of a former hostage who says she was sexually assaulted while in captivity, initially while chained by the ankle, and in a child's bedroom decorated in a SpongeBob SquarePants motif.

The divisions that existed before this war have become toxically entrenched. Hostilities have spread around the world, and we are certainly seeing this in Canada.

The other day, in a social media thread about a Vancouver soap store selling watermelon dishcloths to raise money for aid in Gaza, a commenter suggested that the store should also be supporting the return of the hostages. In response, another user posted a yawn emoji. This is where we are.

If hope can be found anywhere at this point, it's in Israeli–Palestinian groups such as Women Wage Peace (WWP) and Standing Together, which advocate for peace and equality. Since October 7th, interest in their work has surged globally, and both are now active in Canada: representatives from Standing Together were in Toronto this week for a public event, and earlier this month, WWP held its inaugural online gathering for Canadian supporters. Both groups are facing the fight of their lives.

WWP is already well-known in Canada as the organization co-founded by Vivian Silver.

"We all loved Vivian . . . and we continue in her footsteps," WWP's Regula Alon told the attendees. "It's her legacy."

At the event, a video was screened of Ms. Silver speaking to a crowd in Jerusalem in September 2021. "We all deserve a better life," she said in Hebrew.

Women Wage Peace was founded after the 2014 war in Gaza to declare "with one voice, enough! to the failed paradigm of endless managed conflict," its website states. The multi-faith WWP signed an agreement with the Palestinian women's peace group Women of the Sun in 2022. They named it "The Mothers' Call."

We "believe there is another way," Ms. Alon, who is part of WWP's foreign relations team, told the interested Canadians.

Standing Together, another group made up of Israeli Jews and Palestinians, believes this, too.

"We need a different approach," Rula Daood, a Palestinian Israeli who lives in Jaffa and serves as the group's national co-director, told me in an interview. "We need different politics. We need to end the occupation; we need to bring freedom and equality to both people. That is the only way we can achieve real prosperity for everybody living in Israel/Palestine. And I do think we have an opportunity right now and we need to seize it."

The event was sponsored by the New Israel Fund of Canada, which, according to its website, supports a "just and democratic Israel that upholds equality for all its citizens."

In his introduction at the Toronto Reference Library, the fund's director Ben Murane talked about the visiting group offering "a small candle of hope that Jews and Palestinians can stand together" and "a hopeful antidote to the despair plaguing us." This amid accelerating division, hate, and one-sided demands for exclusivity of victimhood.

Unlike some in the pro-Palestinian space, Standing Together in no way downplays, denies, or justifies the atrocities of October 7th. But it also says the occupation cannot continue and is strongly opposed to Benjamin Netanyahu. It is calling for an end to the war and the return of the hostages.

"There is a very big difference between being in favour of the people living in Israel and the Israeli government," says Ms. Daood.

"We need to build a society that understands that the benefit of having real peace and real agreement is for both sides. Having peace does not just benefit the Palestinians. It also benefits the people in Israel. Because then you don't have to be in a place where you're scared of your neighbours, where we're at constant wars."

Two days after the October 7th attacks, I wrote that your Jewish and Palestinian friends are not doing okay. I can tell you with great certainty that we are doing much, much worse now. In this ceaseless and dark panorama of death, despair, and polarization, groups like Women Wage Peace and Standing Together offer a different path, bringing in a bit of light and something that feels impossible now: hope, for peace, in spite of it all.

APRIL 19TH, 2024

*One day after a motion to end a ban on the keffiyeh in the
Ontario legislature fails to pass, meaning the traditional
Muslim scarf, which has become an emblem of the
Palestinian cause, remains prohibited.*

Grade twelve students are making big decisions about what comes next. Parents' Facebook feeds feature proud announcements about where their child will attend university in the fall. It's lovely.

But for Jewish parents, a new factor has entered into the mix: Where can we send our kids that will be safe?

Universities have become a flashpoint in the fallout from the Israel–Hamas war. The tension has been palpable on some campuses, including York University, Toronto Metropolitan University (TMU), and Concordia University. Jewish university students have been sworn at and told to "go back to Poland." They have read social media posts by fellow students and faculty that have poisoned the atmosphere. An independent investigator was brought in to deal with a controversial open letter at TMU's law school that declared support for "all forms of Palestinian resistance." In a high-profile hearing in Washington, the House Committee on Education and the Workforce grilled four Columbia University officials, including its president, Minouche Shafik, about antisemitism on campus.

"It's impossible to exist as a Jewish student at Columbia without running face first into antisemitism every single day," read one statement by a student, delivered at the hearing by Republican representative Burgess Owens. "Jew-hatred is so deeply embedded into the campus culture, it's become casual among students, faculty, and neglected by administrators."

Allegations of antisemitism at Columbia include the beating of an Israeli student with a stick. Students say they have been verbally attacked for being Jewish. The committee heard about a School of Social Work orientation guidebook that defines "Ashkenormativity" as "a system of oppression that favors white Jewish folx."

There was also a lot of attention on Joseph Massad, who teaches modern Arab politics at Columbia. Dr. Massad, of Christian Palestinian descent, published an article on October 8th, 2023—the day after Hamas killed more than 1,100 people and took more than 240 hostage—describing the paraglider incursion as "an innovative Palestinian resistance" and using language including "awesome" and "stunning." This was before Israel retaliated with its brutal, deadly war in Gaza.

Mr. Owens, who is Black, suggested there was a double standard at the university, saying that if anyone called an attack on Black people "awesome" and "stunning," it would not be tolerated.

Columbia students set up a Gaza-solidarity encampment on the lawn outside the campus library; protesters' chants included calls for an intifada and support for the Houthis.[1] The university was on lockdown, with barricades and a strong police presence. Police moved in and made arrests.

Protest is essential in a democracy and is often an important, meaningful part of the university experience. But what happens when the tenor and pervasiveness of the protests make others feel unsafe?

Dr. Shafik said that when she first started at Columbia—she became its president last July—its policies and enforcement mechanisms were "not up to the scale of this challenge."

"They were designed for a very different world," she testified.

The hearing may have been well-intentioned, and the explosion of antisemitism on university campuses is certainly worthy of scrutiny. But this was lost at times in the clamour by members of Congress to score political points. They were trying to elicit a gotcha moment, similar to when Harvard's then-president was grilled at a December hearing with other academic leaders. On

---

[1] The Houthis, an Iranian-backed militia group, began attacking commercial ships in the Red Sea in November 2023, in an operation meant to target Israel and its allies.

whether calling for the genocide of Jews is in violation of campus policies, she said, "It can be, depending on the context."

Politicking is not going to fix this. And neither is clamping down on freedoms—which is also happening on campus, and largely affecting pro-Palestinian students.

At the University of Southern California (USC), Asna Tabassum, a biomedical engineering student who is Muslim, lost the honour of speaking as valedictorian this week after pressure from pro-Israeli groups, which complained she has posted anti-Zionist statements. USC cited safety concerns in its decision, saying it had received warnings that the commencement would be disrupted—and that Ms. Tabassum was herself a target.

Silencing her is unacceptable. Why are we letting the mob rule?

The chill is reaching far beyond universities, too. How did we get to a place where the Speaker of the Ontario legislature would ban the keffiyeh—a traditional Palestinian scarf? It's absurd, offensive.

University administrators have a responsibility for student safety, but also student freedoms. They are in a terrible bind, dealing with an out-of-hand situation.

As Dr. Shafik testified, "Trying to reconcile the free-speech rights of those who wanted to protest and the rights of Jewish students to be in an environment free of discrimination and harassment has been the central challenge at our campus and numerous others across the country."

In this country, too.

Jews are a tiny minority in Canada. But it will be interesting to see how these experiences affect enrolment numbers at certain places of higher learning.

POSTSCRIPT: *In May 2024, the external review at TMU ruled that the law school letter was a valid exercise of student expression and did not breach the university's code of conduct. Minouche Shafik resigned as president of Columbia University in August 2024.*

*One day after a pro-Palestinian encampment is
established at the University of Toronto.*

War is hell: Three words, inarguable. Military industrial complex
aside, this is a statement we can all agree on.

The Israel–Hamas war and its consequential global cataclysms
have produced an earful of slogans. Lacking nuance or context,
their meaning is often in the eye (or ear) of the beholder.

"From the river to the sea, Palestine shall be free." Does that
mean freedom from the oppression in the West Bank and the
bloodbath in Gaza, and true equality from one body of water to
the other? Or is it an existential threat? Some—Israelis and Jews
in particular (not all, but many)—hear this as: from the river to
the sea, Palestine will be free of Jews.

Carleton University political science professor Mira Sucharov
said on CBC Radio that she wished the phrase was instead
"Palestinians" shall be free.

"Long live October 7th," a Vancouver protest heard. A cry for resistance? Please. (The speaker was subsequently arrested in a hate speech investigation.)

People on all sides are being accused of being on the wrong side of history. I would suggest that celebrating deaths is a definitive way to choose the wrong side.

"Globalize the intifada." If what they mean is "World, join us in rising up against the oppression we have experienced since the Nakba," instead of a threat against Jewish lives—that's a different story. But that's not what many people hear.

Some people from the pro-Israel side have referred to people advocating for Palestinian rights or speaking out against the war in Gaza as "pro-Hamas" or "pro-terrorist." Come on. Advocating for Palestinians does not make someone in favour of terrorism—nor does it make them antisemitic.

Then there's that word: "Nazi." As catastrophic as Israel's actions in Gaza are, equating them to what the Nazis did is inaccurate and, to many, offensive. Israel is not systematically herding every Palestinian it can find to their death as an end unto itself. Israel's campaign to destroy Hamas has caused horrific civilian deaths. As devastating as this is, that does not necessarily mean it is a genocide. As *The Atlantic*'s Graeme Wood noted, prosecution at the International Court of Justice needs to demonstrate the intent to destroy a protected group. It also must show that there is an absence of plausible non-genocidal intent that could explain Israel's actions.

Why offensive? The word "genocide" was invented during the Second World War to describe the campaign to destroy European Jewry. The global Jewish population has still not recovered.

"Never again," Jews say in reference to the Holocaust. This should not just mean "never again will Jews allow themselves to be shoved into gas chambers while the world yawns and keeps its borders shut tight." "Never again" should mean: no more killing innocent people, no more displacement. How can anyone justify the misery caused to Gazans, as they shuffle from one unsafe place to another, having lost family, limbs, pets, homes, possessions?

Gazan officials say more than thirty-four thousand people have died in the war. Supporters of Israel often counter that those numbers can't be trusted. So what? So what if it's not quite thirty-four thousand? Would we be okay with that?

Not in my name.

At the ballooning campus protests, where people with varying degrees of knowledge of the situation have chosen a side, the clashes have been described as war zones under siege—without a hint of irony.

"All Zionists are racists," I saw on a T-shirt. In my understanding, a Zionist is someone who supports the existence of the State of Israel. That makes most (but not all) Jews Zionists. But it has taken on another connotation; for some, it has become a dirty word. There's a video from Montreal where young people in keffiyehs sing about Zionists being racists. The last line of the altered ditty: "And go back to Europe."

We all know what happened in Europe. Genocide.

For the first post–October 7th Yom HaShoah—Holocaust Remembrance Day—some memorials have been covered over concerns about vandalism, or worse. That week, Poland's Nozyk Synagogue, Warsaw's only pre-war synagogue still standing (the Nazis used it as a stable) was firebombed.

There's a song that Jews all over the world sing during the Passover holiday. "Dayenu" goes through the Passover story, thanking God for each action that freed the Israelites from slavery. "Dayenu" means "it would have been enough."

Enough. It's enough.

Bring them home. Ceasefire now.

POSTSCRIPT: *On the term "genocide," many groups have determined that Israel's actions in Gaza constitute a genocide. They include Amnesty International, Human Rights Watch, the University Network for Human Rights and, as stated earlier, the Raphael Lemkin Institute. This charge is strongly disputed by Israel and supporters including the American Jewish Committee and the Centre for Israel and Jewish Affairs.*

Retired Canadian Supreme Court Justice Rosalie Abella also rejects this terminology. As she wrote in The Globe and Mail *in January, 2024: "Hamas's explicit and unapologetic goal is to eliminate Jews. The elimination of Jews is genocide. That is why Hamas murdered, raped, beheaded, kidnapped and tortured Jews on Oct. 7, 2023: to eliminate them, because* they were Jews. It is a legal absurdity to suggest that a country that is defending itself from genocide is thereby guilty of genocide."

She wrote that genocide, rape and torture are in evidence around the world. And yet it is Israel that is predominantly targeted, accused of this crime.

"As a lawyer, I find it shameful; as a Jew, I find it heartbreaking; and as the child of Holocaust survivors, I find it unconscionable," she wrote.

Her argument really resonated with me.

What do I think? If the definition of genocide is the deliberate killing of people from a particular nation or ethnic group with the aim of destroying that group, then even a deadly war that kills tens of thousands does not necessarily fit that definition. If so, we will have to rewrite history and call nearly every war a genocide.

Massacre? Yes. War crimes? Probably. Catastrophic? Absolutely. Disproportionate response to an attack? I am not a military strategist, but it appears that way.

But is Israel's aim to destroy the entire group?

The United Nations defines genocide as an intent to destroy, in whole or in part, a national, ethnical, racial or religious group by doing any of the following: killing members of the group; causing serious bodily or mental harm to members of the group; deliberately inflicting on the group conditions of life calculated to bring about its physical destruction in whole or in part; imposing measures intended to prevent births within the group; forcibly transferring children of the group to another group.

There are, tragically, checkmarks next to the first four of these, and arguably number five; what is to become of orphaned children? But the question of "intent to destroy" is central to this. Israel's intent is to destroy Hamas. That said, some Israeli officials have made statements about Gaza as a whole that have been interpreted as genocidal. On October 10, 2023, Israel's then-defence minister Yoav Gallant said "Gaza won't return to what it was before. There will be no Hamas. We will eliminate everything."

The sentence "There will be no Hamas" was absent from much of the coverage; I missed it too, until The Atlantic's Yair Rosenberg wrote about mistaken citations in January, 2024. That one phrase is of utmost importance. Without it, it appeared that Israel was vowing to eliminate Gaza, not just Hamas.

Further, this statement was made in anger, shock, horror at what had happened three days earlier. But Nissim Vaturi, deputy speaker of the Knesset, called for Israel to burn Gaza following the attacks. And some Israeli politicians called for blocking deliveries of food and fuel—actions meant to impact not just Hamas operatives, but all Gazans. Children. Pregnant women. Everyone. Still, this was not a pre-planned unprovoked elimination strategy, in the manner of the Nazis of the Second World War, or Hamas, whose founding doctrine states very clearly its intent to destroy Israel.

But this mass (if not total) elimination of Gaza, not just Hamas, did come to be; Gaza is certainly not what it was before. The Palestinian Central Bureau of Statistics reported in January 2025 that the population of Gaza had fallen by six percent since the war began. Absolutely tragic. (Israel disputed this data.) Further, if plans materialize to completely uproot Palestinians from Gaza, that would be a genocidal action.

This is a sickening parsing, I know; a splitting of hairs defining the deaths of actual people. What matters is that the killing must stop.

Israeli air strikes targeting Rafah in late May, killing
Gazans already displaced because of the war, prompt an
urgent meeting of the UN Security Council on May 28th.

All eyes were on Rafah this week, and what happened in the southern Gaza city was very hard on the eyes. And the soul.

"I saw bodies everywhere. Children burning. I saw heads without bodies, the injured running around in pain, some alive but trapped inside burning tents," a lawyer identified as Zuhair told *The Guardian*, after an Israeli air strike at a refugee camp.

The catastrophe is spiralling with justifications and explanations, vengeance and grief, digging giant holes into families and creating a seismic shift in future history.

This should not, and will not, be forgotten. It will live in the bones of survivors and their descendants, and in the descendants of the dead. In the blood memory of two peoples, reverberating around the world.

All of this will make peace—already a shaky proposition—even more difficult to attain.

Benjamin Netanyahu has been a disaster for the Palestinians, long before this war—but also for Israel. The horrific October 7th attacks happened on his watch. Since then, he has failed the hostages, their families, the Israelis he has sent to war and their families, and anyone who cares about the State of Israel. He has fed into a grave existential crisis, attracting the world's fury, destabilizing support from even Israel's greatest allies, and, in the process, inspiring hatred toward not just Israel but Jews in the diaspora, too.

If you think that's blaming the victim, fair. Yes, Israel was a victim on October 7th, and it has been victimized through the decades by hostile neighbours. But it has in turn created victims and continues to do so. Is it Hamas's fault? Sure. And the hostages must be returned. But Israel is now sending the bombs, bullets, and soldiers.

The soldiers themselves are victims of this catastrophic war, in a country where military service is mandatory and reserves have been called up in wartime. However, some of their actions have been grotesque, too. A group of Israeli soldiers filmed themselves burning books, including a Quran, during their operation in Gaza. This is not what this state was established, in the ancient homeland of the Jews after the Holocaust, to become.

It is frustrating to see so much of the world's focus on Israel's actions when there are killing fields in so many other places.

One may surmise that this has something to do with the age-old hatred of Jews. But not talking about Gaza is not going to stop what's happening in Syria, Sudan, the Democratic Republic of the Congo. This doesn't give anyone a pass for antisemitism or for applauding the murderous attacks of October 7th as "resistance."

Hamas knew exactly what it was doing. It got the war it wanted. And with Israel's bombardment of Gaza, it got the international sympathy it needed, using its own people as pawns. Mr. Netanyahu has been offering a giant helping hand to Hamas's dream of eradicating Israel.

Israel has insisted that victory is impossible without taking Rafah. If there's a ceasefire now, some Israel supporters say, the terrorists win.

But nobody is winning. The losses are piling up, along with the bodies. Every death is a disaster. Even if Israel "wins," this war has ignited a much deeper divide—who would have thought that possible?—that will last generations and echo far beyond the Middle East.

How can anyone call anything about this a victory?

Yes, people die—innocent people—in war. Yes, historically it has been "acceptable" to kill members of a declared enemy state. Today our view is more humanitarian, perhaps because we are able to see the evidence immediately. And all eyes can see that none of this is okay.

There is no moral equivalence between Hamas and Israel. But there is no moral victory to be found in the rubble, either.

"They want us dead" is a rationalization from some Israelis and their supporters. Even if that were entirely true, that's no justification. If this started out as defence, it has become offence now, and it's offensive. And these thousands of Palestinian deaths have created chasms of grief—and hatred. A lot more people want Israelis dead now than eight months ago.

The Globe and Mail recently shared the horrific experiences of Hagar Brodutch, who was taken hostage on October 7th with four children and released in November. I'll give her the last word.

"I think Israel has to stop everything and bring everybody back home, and that's it," Ms. Brodutch told *The Globe* in Toronto. "Stop the war. I want to live in peace. I want my kids to have a normal life. They have to find a solution for us and for the Palestinians. It can't go on like this."

JUNE 5TH, 2024

One day before Israeli air strikes target a school sheltering
displaced Palestinians in Gaza, killing more than thirty people.
Israel says Hamas militants were operating out of the school.

There was only one book for sale on Miriam Libicki's table at the Vancouver Comic Arts Festival (VanCAF). *But I Live: Three Stories of Child Survivors of the Holocaust* is a collaborative project pairing graphic novelists with survivors, telling their stories in poignant detail.

Days after the event, VanCAF announced it was banning Ms. Libicki from future events in a statement referencing "important public safety concerns" about an "exhibitor" and her prior role in the Israeli army. The board apologized "for the harm we have caused by our negligence" in allowing her to participate.

While Ms. Libicki was not named in the post, it was clearly about her. The U.S.-Israeli artist, now a permanent Canadian resident, volunteered for the Israeli army in 2000. Two months into her service (as a secretary), the Second Intifada began. She tells the story in her autobiographical comic *Jobnik!* VanCAF's statement came out on a Friday, as Ms. Libicki was preparing Shabbat dinner for family and friends who had travelled to the Vancouver area for her daughter's bat mitzvah, taking place the next day.

After that weekend, Ms. Libicki's lawyer sent a cease-and-desist letter to VanCAF, claiming defamation and human-rights violations. The statement disappeared from the website. Then on June 2nd, VanCAF issued a formal apology.

VanCAF did not respond to several emails; it does not list its board members on its website, and neither statement was signed by an actual name. I attempted to contact VanCAF director Jarrett Evan Samson, who has reportedly stepped down, but was unsuccessful.

But here, briefly, is what happened, according to Ms. Libicki: In 2022, two young women dropped by her table, where she was selling her work, including *Jobnik!* and another autobiographical book with IDF content, *Toward a Hot Jew.* The women asked if the books were anti-Zionist.

Ms. Libicki answered that they were not. Before she could say anything else, the women left.

Ms. Libicki later learned that the women aggressively expressed their concerns about her to a volunteer.

Fast-forward two years to 2024 and Ms. Libicki was told by VanCAF not to sell those books or display IDF imagery at her table.

"It is definitely a double standard," she said in an interview. "They're not checking the national origin of other cartoonists."

She sold *But I Live*, some zines, and T-shirts. But the same two women, according to Ms. Libicki, complained about her and things escalated.

The following Friday, VanCAF issued its "accountability post," unsigned, criticizing itself for "the oversight and ignorance to allow this exhibitor in the festival," and saying that having the artist attend the event disregarded "all of our exhibiting artists, attendees and staff, especially those who are directly affected by the ongoing genocide in Palestine and Indigenous community members alike."

"I'm dangerous to Indigenous people also?" Ms. Libicki says. "It was super, super upsetting to see that announcement. And it was really hard to have it not colour my whole weekend and focus on my daughter. She worked so hard, working for months to prepare for her bat mitzvah."

Ms. Libicki had been a VanCAF exhibitor since 2012, when she attended with that same daughter, then not quite two weeks old. She has a lot of friends and admirers in the comics community, and many made their displeasure known to VanCAF. Members of the Jewish community also chimed in.

With little information, it appeared that Ms. Libicki was being banned for serving in the Israeli army. She did so voluntarily, but military service is compulsory for most Israelis—so such a ban would effectively discriminate against Israelis based on nationality.

After the backlash, VanCAF's subsequent "formal apology" explained that the safety concerns were instigated by "activists protesting the individual's presence at the festival" and that Ms. Libicki (unnamed) posed no security threat. "We should never have allowed this individual to be scapegoated like this."

It is vindication for Ms. Libicki, but not enough. "Once you defamed somebody, you can't really take it back and I won't really know the long-term consequences."

Ms. Libicki would like some sort of formal and public reconciliation process to take place with VanCAF, whoever they are. And sensitivity training.

Just imagine if the unnamed organizers of VanCAF had taken a breath, given things some thought, reached out to Ms. Libicki before publicly shaming her.

With Israel and Hamas at war, there has been so much screaming at one another, across a widening divide. What could be accomplished by having actual conversations?

This isn't the only instance of selective targeting of Israeli, Jewish, or Palestinian artists by arts organizations. With festival and awards season approaching in the fall, there is reason to fear more exclusions to come.

One day after Benjamin Netanyahu delivers a fiery speech
to U.S. Congress, condemning U.S. protests and vowing
to press on until Israel's "total victory."

Among Canadian literary awards, the Scotiabank Giller Prize is the big kahuna: the best known and the biggest monetary prize available exclusively to a Canadian author. It also has a quantifiable impact on book sales.

That reputation has been tarnished because of recent events that have nothing to do with Canadian literature, the prize, or its recipients. I'm not sure how, moving forward, there can ever be a Giller Prize without an asterisk. And what a loss that is.

Those protesting will say that the diminishment of the prize is nothing compared with the gutting losses in Gaza. They're right, of course.

But what good can targeting a Canadian literary prize do in terms of ending a horrific overseas war?

The problem is the Giller's sponsor, Scotiabank—specifically its investments in Elbit Systems, an Israeli weapons manufacturer.

This first became clear when protesters infiltrated the swanky Giller ceremony—and live TV broadcast—last November. Some two thousand authors signed an open letter calling for charges against those protesters to be dropped.

A new open letter has been signed by potential 2024 Giller nominees, saying they will not submit their work for consideration. Some past nominees and winners also signed.

The letter demands not only that the prize drop its relationship with Scotiabank, but that the Giller Foundation use its "organizational leverage" to pressure Scotiabank to fully divest from Elbit (which perhaps overestimates how much sway a literary prize has over a bank's investment decisions).

It also demands the organization cut ties with Indigo, the Azrieli Foundation, and Audible, "all sponsors who are actively invested in Israel's ongoing genocide of Palestinians."

Audible is problematic because it is owned by Amazon, which partners with the tech company Palantir, whose chief executive, the letter states, supports Israel's military actions in Gaza.

So where is the open letter against the Amazon Canada First Novel Award? (As it turns out, Audible says it is no longer a sponsor of the Giller, which the letter was amended to acknowledge.)

If Indigo is such a problem (the bookstore chain is controlled by Gerald Schwartz and Heather Reisman, who fund a scholarship for non-Israelis who enlist with the Israeli army), then why allow your publisher to continue to sell your books there?

Ms. Reisman is also criticized for donating to Hillel, which provides on-campus support to Jewish post-secondary students (who have never needed support more). Hillel also fights anti-semitism on campus (ditto).

As for the Azrieli Foundation, its main work in books has been publishing memoirs of Canadian Holocaust survivors. It also funds prizes and grants in music, architecture, and science. Some of the institutions it funds are in Israel.

Its founder, a Holocaust survivor himself, fought for Israel in the 1948 War of Independence, also known as the Nakba, which is called out by the letter.

"As long as the Giller Foundation continues to receive funding from ANY sponsors who are directly invested in Israel's occupation of Palestine, it will still be complicit in genocide."

So if those are the rules, what about other prize funders?

I recently received an upbeat email from the Carol Shields Prize for Fiction announcing various initiatives. Its main sponsor is Bank of Montreal. A quick Google search tells me that the bank is on the "shame list" of the Canadian BDS Coalition, which says BMO has investments in Israeli settlements, citing the Dutch organization BankTrack.

If that's the case, are authors also withdrawing their books from consideration for that prize?

Whataboutism can be a futile exercise. But here's a terrible thing: There are people who suspect the Giller is being targeted not just because of its sponsor, but because the prize was founded by a philanthropist named Jack Rabinovitch and is now run by his daughter, Elana Rabinovitch. Rabinovitch is an obviously Jewish name.

I personally know some of the people who have signed that letter, and I am certain they are not antisemitic. But this is where we are.

In any case, imagine what these corporations that dump all this money into cultural prizes are thinking right now. They do it for a variety of reasons, some more self-serving than others, but certainly among them is the goodwill it generates for their brand. So why send their people into these ceremonies to be booed and humiliated? Why pay all this money to receive the opposite of goodwill?

My fear is these companies will pick up their toys (and cash) and go home. Who loses? The artists (and publishers) who could use the financial and promotional boost. Also the readers, who will lose exposure to good Canadian books.

The corporations will find other things to do with their billions, or perhaps leave more money in their coffers—more dividends for their shareholders.

As for the Giller, it appears to be in disarray. Two jurors have withdrawn. The criticism has gained a lot of traction.

And whoever wins this year, if the prize does go ahead, will always have that asterisk next to their name. That's a shame. And I don't know how it will help the people of Gaza.

POSTSCRIPT: *In announcing its 2024 longlist, the Giller Prize dropped the name "Scotiabank" from the award's title. Organizers said it wanted to ensure the focus remained on the prize and the art itself. But protests against the prize by authors, including some past winners, continued, including outside the ceremony itself, where protesters yelled "shame" as attendees arrived. The ceremony, in a change from previous years, was not broadcast live. Anne Michaels won the award for her novel* Held. *In her speech, which attracted some intense criticism, she called for unity in the arts. In February 2025, The Giller Foundation announced an early end to its partnership with Scotiabank, effective immediately.*

One day after the Israeli military announces that it killed the
head of Hamas's military wing in a July air strike in Gaza.

The intersection of the LGBTQ and Jewish communities has been jammed with heartache since October 7th. There has been heartache in all communities affected by the Israel–Hamas war, of course. But there is a real feeling of betrayal among some gay Jewish Canadians.

"You think you understand your place in your community and then your whole world is flipped upside down, and you are now shown that everything is not as what it seemed and that your membership is conditional," says Torontonian Shoshannah Cooper-Porter, who describes herself as "unapologetically" Black, Jewish, and queer. "I am grieving."

There is shock, anger, and a disorienting incredulousness that they no longer feel welcome in spaces that used to feel safe, such as Pride events.

"Pride feels different for me," wrote Helen Sadeh in an Instagram post ahead of Toronto's parade. "I have been watching the LGBTQ community turn its collective back on my boys." Ms. Sadeh, a Sephardic Jew living just north of Toronto, has three teenage sons, all of whom are gay. Her husband was born in Israel and came to Canada as a baby.

"It is sad to see that the LGBTQ community, who prides itself on pride of being who you are in every aspect, is so overtly exclusive in this regard," she said in an interview this week. "It hurts."

A Jewish contingent marched in Toronto's Pride Parade; it included the Sadehs. At the same time, some long-time Jewish participants decided to skip it this year. Security for the group was tight: one security person for every two expected participants, according to the Centre for Israel and Jewish Affairs (CIJA). There was a warm reception from the crowd along the way, participants I spoke to said. But the group also encountered boos, middle fingers, and aggressive signs and jeers.

"It takes a very hideous person to yell at queer and trans folks who are marching in a Pride parade," says Jess Burke, DEI director and training liaison to 2SLGBTQIA+ partnerships with CIJA. Ms. Burke, who is a lesbian married to an Israeli, says a security diversion had to be enacted as the group ended its march because of counter-protesters who she says were harassing and pursuing them.

"I think it opened up people's eyes to see what it's like to be queer and Jewish right now," she told me.

The parade was ultimately shut down by pro-Palestinian protesters. (I struggle with this term, "pro-Palestinian," because many of the gay Jewish people I spoke to about this [some off the record] are pro-Palestinian; they are for Palestinian rights and want the war to end. But they are rattled by a response they feel veers into antisemitism.)

"It's become rather hostile to the point where we avoid the traditional Pride events that are being put on by the community because we don't feel psychologically or physically safe," a Jewish drag queen who goes by Gila Münster told me this week. (Her signature show is the *8 Gays of Channukah*.) She sat out the parade in Kingston, where she is going into her second year of law school at Queen's, and says she and her partner have lost many friends.

"People we used to think were allies have decided because we are Jewish or because I was born in Israel that we are somehow against the queer community's goal," she said. For her, she says, being queer and Jewish go hand in hand. (Ms. Münster's website features a photo of her in drag wearing an IDF uniform—which would certainly be triggering for some.)

"In law school we're taught how to argue things. But you can't argue with people who are not interested in seeing you as human. It's been dehumanizing to have a story that isn't mine thrust upon me without an opportunity to speak back against it," she says, calling it ungenerous and unfair. "And I don't think that it speaks to the spirit of the Pride movement."

Pride started as a protest movement by the gay community, which has been horribly oppressed. Even if, happily, the event has become celebratory, protest remains at the heart of Pride and the right to protest is sacrosanct.

One does wonder, though, why there is so much focus on protesting this particular war when the parade has not been stopped over other conflicts or wars. As many people I spoke to pointed out, Israel is ironically a haven in the Middle East for LGBTQ people.

In the past, I have attended the Vancouver parade as an ally. My son has also participated (with his dad, another ally). It has always been a joyous, sweaty affair. And important.

This year, I will not be there.

SEPTEMBER 3RD, 2024

*Two days after tens of thousands of Israelis take to the streets
in protest after six more hostages are found dead in Gaza. The
dead include Israeli American Hersh Goldberg-Polin, whose
parents had spoken the previous week to the U.S. Democratic
National Convention, calling for the release of the remaining
hostages and an end to the suffering of innocent Gazans. On
September 2nd, Hamas releases videos of the now-dead hostages.
Israel says the hostages were shot at close range and died one or
two days before Israeli troops reached the tunnel under Rafah
where they were being held on August 31st.*

An open letter to Benjamin Netanyahu:

Sir, this is addressed to you and not the Hamas leadership
because, while they are solely responsible for the abduction and
murders of the hostages—including the six killed last week—
they are despicable, and they are not going to end this. You have
the power to do so.

Further, they are a terrorist group while you are a democratically elected leader (if one who has engaged in queasy political alliances with extremist parties to stay in power). And so, Bibi (if we may), this missive goes out to you.

First of all, mazel tov. It's not every person who can bring so many Jews together (we are a notoriously argumentative bunch) with a shared sentiment. You've done it.

You brought hundreds of thousands of Israelis into the streets in an eruption of grief and anger this weekend; the largest protests to date since this war began, nearly eleven months ago now.

Going back to October 7th, the horrific attacks happened on your watch, a massive military failure. Israel is now fighting one of its longest, deadliest wars.

We know more about the six souls shot at close range in a tunnel under Rafah last week than we do about the thousands of Gazans who have been killed in this war, above ground. Thousands. And yet you persist.

Your defence minister has reportedly urged you to accept concessions in order to reach a deal. U.S. president Joe Biden says you are not doing enough to free the hostages. A huge swath of Israelis agree, including union leaders who called a (short-lived) general strike.

Not sure if you heard the people yelling outside your party headquarters: "Why are they still in Gaza?"

Families of the hostages have begged you to prioritize a deal to allow them to go free. "My boy is still alive!" Einav Zangauker,

mother of hostage Matan Zangauker and previously a supporter of your leadership (no longer), told one of the protests.
"But each passing day is like a Russian roulette that Netanyahu
is playing."[1]

Still, you were defiant, saying that offering concessions now
would be rewarding the slaughter of hostages. You said the end of
the war would come "when Hamas no longer rules Gaza."

The situation for Palestinians in the West Bank is also dire,
as your occupation continues.

Your current path is an existential threat.

Under your watch, world antisemitism has ballooned. Sure, it
appears to have been lurking precipitously close to the surface,
but thanks for offering the prick that allowed it to explode.
Apologies if this feels like victim blaming, but this will be part of
your legacy, we're afraid. We are afraid.

Israel could be a progressive state working on a two-state
solution, which you are on record as opposing. Instead, it has
become an international pariah.

We think of those six hostages waiting days, weeks, months
for rescue, including Israeli American Hersh Goldberg-Polin,
twenty-three, who lost part of his left arm in the October 7th
attacks. Instead, they were shot dead. Have you seen the videos

---

[1] During a February 2025 release of three other hostages under the
ceasefire agreement, Hamas displayed an onstage photo of Matan
Zangauker, still being held hostage, along with a photo of his mother,
next to an image of an hourglass and a warning: "Time is running out."

of those poor souls, which Hamas posted after murdering them? If so, how do you sleep?

We think of the Palestinian children who have also had limbs blown off in this brutal war. We think of the families in Gaza who are displaced and grieving. We think of the starving, desperate innocents.

Polio has returned to Gaza; it could spread far beyond. (Thank you, though, for allowing the pause in your war to administer polio vaccines. Perhaps this will put an end to the use of the term "genocide" to describe your massacre. Doubt it, though.)

You have let heartbreak reign. All over the world, we are sitting shiva on Facebook and X, on FaceTime calls with faraway friends. We are fighting among ourselves, trying to determine the best way forward. We have all become armchair military analysts. We are too sad to describe with words.

Way over here in Vancouver on Sunday, freshly hand-drawn signs offered apologies to Mr. Goldberg-Polin and Carmel Gat, who has family in Canada. "Sorry we couldn't save you," they said.

Online, we have seen a photo of Mr. Goldberg-Polin's bedroom with the poster over his desk declaring "Jerusalem is everyone's" in English, Arabic, and Hebrew.

At his funeral, his mother, Rachel, stood in front of thousands and spoke directly to her son. "Okay, sweet boy, go now on your journey. I hope it's as good as the trips you dreamed about because finally, my sweet boy, finally, finally, finally, finally you are free."

His father, also in a ripped T-shirt denoting mourning, apologized. "We all failed you," Jon Polin said. He added, "Maybe your death is the stone, the fuel, that will bring home the 101 other hostages."

Prime Minister, make it so.

OCTOBER 7TH, 2024

As Israelis, Palestinians, Jews, Muslims and others around the world mark the anniversary, the war continues to rage, with both Hamas and Hezbollah firing rockets into Israel and Israel mounting air strikes on Lebanon and Gaza.

A year can feel like forever, and it can go by in a flash. This has been a forever year. With a grim anniversary upon us, an end to what has made it feel so awfully endless seems very far away with only more ahead: escalation, displacement, death. Fear, of the existential variety.

On October 7th, 2023, the day of the Hamas attacks, it seemed inevitable that Israel would retaliate and things would be terrible. But this terrible? A *year* terrible? This-many-thousands-of-deaths terrible? Now war on several fronts? Not even I, glass-half-empty doomsayer with intergenerational trauma in my bones, would have predicted this.

Nor would I have predicted the extent to which the horrors of that day have rippled, affecting Canadian schools, universities, hospitals, sporting events, film festivals, bookstores. Boycotts, vandalism, infighting.

I never thought I would have to call my son's beloved former principal to ask about social media posts regarding Vancouver elementary school children taking part in a pro-Palestinian protest. (He never responded.)

I never thought I would need to send emails to a local theatre about antisemitic "jokes" made on its stage. (They never responded.)

Our pain is barely acknowledged—or worse.

I would not have predicted that my camera roll would turn into a jumble of screenshots: upsetting things shared, liked—or written—by politicians, artists, academics, union leaders, progressives. Rape denial, antisemitic tropes. And then that Jews would be told that what they are experiencing is not actually antisemitism. The gaslighting has been something else. If such things were said about any other community, they would never be tolerated.

I never would have predicted that to mark the anniversary of the brutal murders in Israel—of small children and elderly Holocaust survivors and everyone in between, the kidnappings, rapes, burnings of homes and possessions—people in this country would hold events celebrating the "resistance." The absolute gall.

Incidents of antisemitism and Jewish-targeted hate crimes have soared in Canada, where Jews are a tiny percentage of the population. On a Toronto Jewish Facebook group, a woman shared a story about the protest targeting the Giller Prize and wrote: "Please. Leave us alone."

That's how it feels—the protests outside Jewish restaurants, synagogues, community centres, including one across the street from a Jewish seniors' home in Ottawa last month. Please, leave us alone.

I am no fan of Benjamin Netanyahu, and I am anti-war. I am for peace. And yet the cold hostility directed my way has been palpable. Why? Because I believe that a State of Israel has a right to exist. From the other "side," I have been charged with betraying the Jewish people for calling out a catastrophic war. Because I believe Palestinians deserve safety and security and their own country.

I am pro-Palestinian and Jewish. This is not an oxymoron.

I could write a million words on the politics—how proxies for Iran are targeting Israel, how frightening this should be for a democratic world, how Mr. Netanyahu has put Israel under threat in part to protect his own interests—but I am stuck on the grief. This anniversary is not reigniting the fear and the heartbreak, the anguish and bitterness; these have become our consistent companions.

We are in the High Holiday period of the Jewish calendar— Rosh Hashanah, the Jewish New Year, was last week, followed by Yom Kippur, which begins Friday evening. We usually wish one another "a sweet year." How to do that as bombs are falling? Outside synagogues across Canada, congregants are greeted by heavy security and police. What is sweet about any of this?

I can't imagine the pain of the hostages who have been held for 366 days in this, the longest leap year. The pain of their families. Of friends and families of those who have been killed in Gaza, Lebanon, Israel.

Safely out of the line of fire, diasporic communities—Jewish, Muslim, Israeli, Palestinian—have been living with this heaviness. The pain has become familiar, a baseline. Now, we welcome our Lebanese brothers and sisters into this unwanted fold. Grief, everywhere.

A rabbi I know shared a graphic that has been circulating in Israel this Rosh Hashanah: the yellow ribbon, a symbol for the release of the hostages, twisted into the Hebrew word *shana* (year). It says "A year without words."

I wish I could write my heart's demand—"No more lives lost!"—and make it so. Alas, nobody has this power. Even the powerful don't seem to have this power, or desire that particular outcome.

There are no words. And yet the only thing many of us can do is use them: to write, to talk to one another. And to express hope for peace, in spite of it all.

There have been angry protests for days, and mournful vigils. I have attended nothing, staying close to home, protecting—it, us. There was a heavy feeling all weekend. On Friday night, the first of the Jewish New Year, I invited my Vancouver Jews, as I call them, over for a Shabbat potluck. It was my only Rosh Hashanah gathering this year; it was all I could handle. (Also, nobody invited me.) I made a brisket, tended to it for hours. The leftovers, all gone now.

In Vancouver at a pro-Palestinian protest tonight, the crowd cheered after the speaker standing on the steps of the beautiful Vancouver Art Gallery called for death to Canada, the U.S., and Israel. In Ottawa, a man, denied access to Parliament Hill during an anti-Israel rally, was told, "If you are not a supporter of Palestine, you are not permitted." In Montreal, pro-Palestinian protesters smashed windows at McGill University.

There were versions of these October 7th anniversary protests all over the world, in New York, Paris, Rome, London. My beloved Dublin. So many places I have loved, where I would not have felt comfortable on these grim days.

I am no longer shocked by anything. But I still find it deeply troubling that the anniversary of people being butchered could become an occasion for protest against those same people. My people. *People.*

My heart has been pounding, reading the coverage. My soul weeping, reading the stories of the savagery that happened one year ago today in a faraway land that I was taught from birth to love. My anger is intensifying, and that scares me. Fear and anxiety, my new baseline, are also intensifying, as antisemitism rears its ever-more-familiar head all around.

This evening I sat at my kitchen counter with a slice of home-baked challah made by a friend, a piping-hot piece of the lasagna made by another—a hug in a pan—and a very large cold glass of wine left over from Friday night. The radio was on; an interview with a mother whose son, her only child, had been murdered on October 7th, 2023, at the Nova Music Festival. An aspiring DJ, he loved to travel. He was planning a trip around the world. He made people feel loved, was completely accepting. He was very tall, a gentle giant, very funny. He was twenty.

She was planning to bury his ashes on the anniversary at sunset, she said, by the roots of a tree they would plant in the Israeli desert, where he lived. They were going to play the lullaby she sang to him when he was a child.

Tomorrow my son turns sixteen.

I have tried to approach this nightmare from what I began to call the humanitarian middle. More important to me than ideology and land are the people who are suffering. More than a Jewish person, a journalist, someone who was brought up to love Israel, a child of Holocaust survivors, I am a human being, a mother, who cares about other human beings. The responses to my October 7th anniversary column were predictable: an outpouring of empathy and gratitude from people who are walking the same path as me, including the path of the newly ideologically homeless, as I have come to think of it.

And there was hate, too, of course. And ignorance. One guy wrote to me that we are on the brink of World War Three, which will forever be known as the war caused by the Jews. Another person called me a rancid whore, told me to rot in hell. (He didn't like what I had previously written about a Russian film.) Someone wrote on X, "Do you have a pager or walkie talkie?" This was a reference to the Israeli operation targeting members of Hezbollah with exploding devices.

There was a lot of silence.

It's become normal for me this year, this hatred. One afternoon, I was at the pharmacy picking up some allergy medication for my son when I made the mistake of checking my phone. Someone on social media was calling for me to be sent to The Hague, presumably to be tried for war crimes. This person was decrying something I had written that week; "disgusting," she called it. It was the column stating that protests don't belong outside hospitals.

Which they do not.

If you do the job that I am very fortunate to have, you are going to get a lot of reader mail. You are going to get a lot of awful mail, in addition to blistering posts on social media and belittling comments left online, attached to the stories themselves.

This war escalated the volume and the vitriol.

I have been called a "genocidal monster," "an appalling, piece of shit genocide-supporting lunatic," "a Zionist stooge." A racist. A Nazi.

Imagine being a child of Holocaust survivors and being called a Nazi.

People wrote to me about God and Satan. Others emailed missives about the evils of religion. I was sent quotes from the Bible.

"Your stupidity astounds on every level," someone wrote to me. Stop cheering for Israeli monsters murdering children, I was told. "You are absolute trash, another lying journalist." How dare I write about feelings of "Jew university students," one person inquired. I was called an enabler; I was accused of "celebrating" the suffering of Palestinians.

I have also been called a traitor to the Jewish people. "Your one-sided approach gives rise to antisemitism," someone wrote to me.

"I would feel ashamed if I were a child of survivors and wrote this article for everyone to see," a woman emailed in response to the column that began with "Hatikvah," the hope. Another woman wrote that she was profoundly hurt by this column.

"Your article was another punch in the stomach for me as a Jewish person, the mother and grandmother of Jewish children. And so, I was devastated after reading it."

In particular, many Jewish readers were unhappy with the long piece which first ran online November 10th , 2023 and in print on November 11th, Remembrance Day, with the headline "Why do people hate Israel so much?"

One reader was very upset that her children had to see that headline. "You are hurting Jews," she wrote.

The subject line to one email read "You're never happy." (This writer was not far off.)

Another writer, months into the war, called me an "evil self-hating Jew" who used my status as a child of Holocaust survivors as a shield to attack Israel and other Jews. "So go to hell, you assimilated ignorant anti-Semitic witch. Leave us alone already, you have no future among the Jewish people," the person wrote.

There was one person who emailed me repeatedly in response to a wide array of subjects I wrote about in *The Globe* over that year, taking me to task for not sufficiently condemning the war in Gaza. A column about why air conditioning should no longer be considered a frill in Canada as temperatures rise? Well, it's pretty hot in Gaza, he scolded me. When I wrote about immature behaviour in the House of Commons, he sent me a note outraged that I would care about decorum rather than taking a stand against what Israel was doing.

Would another (i.e., non-Jewish) journalist be targeted that way?

I share these responses to present some idea of the range and depth of feelings people have about this. The anger, sorrow, desperation. If only the act of writing angry letters to me could actually accomplish something about the man-made calamity in the Middle East.

There is something about human nature: We can be offered thousands of words of encouragement and one scathing insult, and it is the insult that will stick. Perhaps haunting us in the middle of the night, when we can't sleep because the world is so terrible. Perhaps word for word. Instead of counting sheep, darker numbers run through our brains, darker words. *Genocidal monster.*

But something unusual happened to me over the first year of writing about this catastrophe. I was able to focus on other comments; buoyed by reader mail, often excruciatingly emotional, that urged me to keep going. (Even if I was often too busy to reply.) *You are representing a point of view I share. Nuanced, rational. Keep writing, please.*

"Yours is one of the few voices that mirrors what I'm feeling post–October 7th as a Jewish person," someone wrote to me. Many of the writers were not Jewish and said they appreciated my perspective; that they were upset by the rise in antisemitism, but also expressed grave concerns about the Palestinians (which I share, let me repeat; these two viewpoints are not mutually exclusive).

I have worked in journalism long enough to know that my little voice cannot make a difference in the outcome of this enormous conflict. Benjamin Netanyahu and the leaders of Hamas were not listening to me. But I have also seen that I was able to provide some solace for others who were, like me, devastated by what they were witnessing and experiencing—including Jewish people who were conflicted between stories they grew up with and what they were seeing with their own eyes, and who were rocked by the antisemitism that was allowed to rise, once again. And the gaslighting that accompanied that rise.

It has been a terrible time. But I can write these words in safety from the (air-conditioned) comfort of *The Globe and Mail*'s B.C. bureau, with its large windows, fancy coffee machine, and generous colleagues—where I often worked on this collection.

One Saturday afternoon, as I was writing some of these words, I could hear a pro-Palestinian protest, about a block away. These had been going on for months. The next day, there was to be another "bring them home" gathering for the Israeli hostages, in the same place. These had also been going on for months. Every weekend, they gathered; I sat alone and wrote. All of us, suffering.

The year is ending; the war is not. The protests will not.

My writing will not.

One woman signed an email to me "in despair." Yes.

The despair will survive generations. The reverberations will be felt long after this time, long after we are gone. These events that have emptied families will fill history books. The sorrow will live in our peoples' bones.

On the first anniversary of the October 7th massacre, I listened to a radio interview in the afternoon on the public broadcaster, a nearly twelve-minute anti-Israel rant by a UBC adjunct professor, who downplayed the Hamas attacks, which went almost completely unchallenged. "We don't need to have alligator's tears," he said. You put this guy on today of all days?

There is a candle in my window tonight.

Tomorrow I will get up and brew coffee, wrap soccer-related gifts for a kid now old enough to drive, order trays of sushi for a birthday dinner.

I will watch a political debate; I will write something about the upcoming provincial election. I will pick up a cake, some milk and eggs, and do a few loads of laundry. If there's time, I'll refill a prescription at the drugstore (high blood pressure).

I get to go on and live my life, with all of its joys and mundanities, with its healable heartbreaks.

How many people have been robbed of this? How many more will join them tomorrow? And the next day, and the next.

Sometimes I feel the weight of the world in my fingers. But the real weight is that no matter what I do with them, no matter what I type, it won't bring an end to this madness. The deaths, the devastation, the hatred that has continued will continue. The consequences we cannot yet foresee. I despair, and yet.

Shalom. Salaam. Peace.

ACKNOWLEDGMENTS

Thank you to *The Globe and Mail* for supporting this project. *The Globe* has given me the gift of being able to write for a large, curious readership—and the freedom to do so with my heart.

Special thanks to Opinion editor Natasha Hassan and deputy editor Mark Medley, as well as to Sarah Efron, Adrian Lee, and Kate Wilkinson, who edited most of these pieces.

Thank you to *Globe Arts* editors over the years, including Judith Pereira, Craig Offman, Jared Bland, Gabe Gonda, and Andrew Gorham.

Thank you to David Walmsley, Sinclair Stewart, and Wendy Cox for their wisdom and humane leadership. And to Doug Tripp for facilitating this project.

Thank you to *The Globe* journalists whose reporting on the war and its many ramifications has been essential reading.

My *Globe* colleagues have been extremely supportive, wise, and caring through difficult times. Special thanks to Nancy Macdonald,

Wendy Stueck, Andrea Woo, Gary Mason, Dave Ebner, Mike Hager, Brent Jang, Nathan VanderKlippe, Ming Wong, André Picard, Simon Houpt, Kate Taylor, Kelly Nestruck, Barry Hertz, Rebecca Tucker, and Stephanie Chambers. Judith Pereira's frequent check-ins have been a godsend.

Thank you to Moira Dann, the then-*Globe* editor who accepted "Going Home to Auschwitz" way back in 1998 and has never stopped cheering me on.

This book would not exist if it weren't for Haley Cullingham, who had the original vision for this project and made it happen under a very compressed deadline. She then thoughtfully and sensitively edited the collection, all while handling my various breakdowns throughout. A huge thank you to Stephanie Sinclair for her enthusiastic support and leadership. Thank you as well to my agent, Martha Webb. I am so fortunate to work with these smart, strong women.

At M&S, thank you to Kimberlee Kemp, Sharon Klein, Rebecca Rocillo, Talia Abramson, Sarah Howland, Tonia Addison, Bree Duwyn, Anita Chong. Thank you to the sensitivity reader for a candid and passionate assessment. Thank you to Sheila Kay.

Thank you to Rosalie Abella, Jon Allen and Ben Murane.

For the photo (and encouragement), thank you to Ben Nelms.

I cannot adequately express my appreciation for friends and family who have offered support, visits, and the occasional lasagna (thank you, Kathryn Gretsinger). Thanks to Tara McGuire for the conversations about writing (and everything else). Special gratitude to my son, Jacob, who puts up with having a workaholic mother and who is a constant reminder of why all of this is so important.

To the many people who have spoken to me about the situation in the Middle East (and Canada), shared personal stories, and trusted me—sometimes warily, understandably—thank you. To the readers who have reached out with heartfelt thoughts and opinions, I appreciate it very much, even if I don't always have the bandwidth to reply.

To the writers and analysts who have shed so much light on the situation and allowed me to use their words, thank you.

For everyone working to bring peace to the Middle East, fighting for humanity, security, safety, health, dignity—and for life itself—"thank you" feels insufficient.

Todah. Shukran.